KARL HOLL

What Did LUTHER Understand by RELIGION?

Edited by
James Luther Adams and Walter F. Bense

Translated by
Fred W. Meuser and Walter R. Wietzke

Ƒ FORTRESS PRESS   Philadelphia

This book is a translation of the essay, "Was verstand Luther unter Religion?" found in Karl Holl, *Gesammelte Aufsätze zur Kirchengeschichte*, Volume 1, pp. 1–110 (Tübingen: J.C.B. Mohr [Paul Siebeck], 7th ed., 1948) and is printed here with the permission of that publisher.

The essay, "Gogarten's Understanding of Luther," translated by Walter F. Bense, was published originally in *Die Christliche Welt*, 38 (1924), cols. 307–314.

Library of Congress Catalog Card Number 76–62611
ISBN 0–8006–1260–4

6184B77   Printed in U.S.A.   1–1260

Contents

iii

Abbreviations

Drews, *Disputationen*	*Disputationen Dr. Martin Luthers,* ed. P. Drews (Göttingen, 1895).
EA	*Sämmtliche Werke in beiden Originalsprachen* . . . , ed. I. K. Irmischer et al. (Frankfurt a. M., 1829ff.).
Enders	*D. Martin Luthers Briefwechsel,* ed. E. L. Enders (Frankfurt a. M., 1884–1923).
GA	Karl Holl, *Gesammelte Aufsätze zur Kirchengeschichte,* vol. 1, *Luther,* 7th ed. (Tübingen, 1948); vol. 2, *Der Osten,* spec. ed. (Darmstadt, 1964); vol. 3, *Der Westen,* spec. ed. (Darmstadt, 1965).
Römerbrief	*D. Martin Luthers Vorlesung über den Römerbrief, 1515/16,* ed. J. Ficker (Leipzig, 1908).
WA	*D. Martin Luthers Werke.* Kritische Gesamtausgabe (Weimar, 1883ff.).
WA, TR	*D. Martin Luthers Werke.* Tischreden (Weimar, 1912–21).
ZThK	*Zeitschrift für Theologie und Kirche.*

Editor's Introduction

The essay that follows this Introduction is based on a public lecture given at the University of Berlin in 1917 in commemoration of the four-hundredth anniversary of the Reformation.[1] Its author, Karl Holl, had been professor of church history at that university since 1906 and, like his older colleague Adolf von Harnack, was better known for his work on the Greek church fathers than on Reformation Protestantism. The approach of these two scholars differed, however. Harnack, in his magisterial *History of Dogma,*[2] seemed to dispose of all dogma in favor of the direct personal influence of the seminal figures of Christian history. Holl's approach was nearly the opposite. Holl began with the personal or "inner" development of the key personalities and tried to show their significance in terms of their relationship to leading ideas—and ultimately, and most specifically, to the idea or concept of God.

When Holl died in 1926 at the age of sixty, he had become one of the best-known Luther-scholars of all time. In his oration at Holl's funeral, Harnack stated that Holl's Luther studies "will remain as long as there is a theological discipline and an evangelical faith, and their author will retain the glory of having become a renewer of Lutheranism."[3] The collection of Holl's Luther studies, first published in 1921, achieved their definitive form with the

---

1. The German text is published in *GA* 1, pp. 1–110, under the title "Was verstand Luther unter Religion?" Many of Holl's footnotes have been shortened or entirely eliminated by the editors, who are responsible for their selection and translation, as well as for paragraph divisions and the seven separately titled sections.
2. Adolf von Harnack, *History of Dogma,* trans. Neil Buchanan et al., 7 vols. (Boston: Little Co., 1903–7; reprinted New York: Russell and Russell, 1958).
3. Adolf von Harnack and Hans Lietzmann, *Karl Holl: Zwei Gedächtnisreden* (Berlin: Walter de Gruyter & Co., 1926), pp. 12–13.

1

second edition of 1923; they are still available in the unchanged seventh edition of 1948.

Holl's renewal of Lutheranism has come to be known as the Luther-Renaissance and was marked by three characteristics, all of them illustrative of the historical method: (1) An unprecedented use of newly available resources for the study of Luther, specifically, the appearance of more and more volumes of the critical Weimar Edition of Luther's works (which made possible the comparison of various versions of Luther's writings and the elimination from the canon of those writings whose authenticity was not demonstrable) and the publication of a number of Luther's early writings previously believed lost. (2) Emphasis on Luther's personal views, their origin and development, rather than on the Lutheran confessional writings and the theology—Lutheran Orthodoxy—based on these confessions. (3) Limited treatment of particular aspects of Luther's thought and work, rather than comprehensive studies of his theology as a whole. This characteristic was due partly to the demands of the historical method for specificity, and partly to Holl's understanding of historiography as the selection of the significant rather than the attempt to reproduce "all" of a past epoch or personality. For all its breadth, therefore, Holl's large Luther volume does not purport to present "the whole Luther," and the present essay is still more limited in its scope.

The opening pages of Holl's essay indicate the three prominent nondogmatic approaches to the study of religion then competing for dominance in Germany—and still competing for dominance almost everywhere today. Of the three, Holl found least congenial the "romantic-mystical" interest in pure feeling and intuition. Holl's objection to this type of religiosity is that it disregards the conscience and the lasting personal relationship to God which he regards as the religious ideal. The second, the history-of-religions approach, was less objectionable to Holl because here the historical material was taken seriously—at least in theory. The individual and unique was recognized as the very stuff of which history is made, and the more reflective advocates of the history-of-religions method acknowledged the significance of the conceptions of God and the conscience inculcated by particular religions. In practice, however, Holl thought that the tendency of this approach was to "look for the typical, the common essence" and then to proclaim this essence as the correct understanding of religion in general. Holl felt closest to the third approach, the philosophical quest for the "psychological preconditions" of religion. This approach, characteristic of serious scholarship through much of the nineteenth century, had discovered not *one common essence* of religion but *two basic types* of religion that differ radically in their psychological preconditions. Kant had identified the egocentric religion of seeking one's own blessedness as a "religion of favor-seeking" and the moral or theocentric religion of transformation into the likeness of the Ideal as a "religion of good conduct." For Kant only the latter was true religion; and within it, he distinguished between a "transformation of the heart" and a more gradual "transformation of morals." Schleiermacher, Hegel, Baur, and Ritschl all followed this approach until Ritschl permitted it to be overshadowed by the quest for blessedness when he discovered the latter's predominance in the religiosity of early Lutheranism, including—as he thought—Luther.[4]

Holl's essay must be understood as directed squarely against Ritschl's understanding of Luther at this point.[5] While Ritschl (following J. C. K. von Hofmann) had sought to distinguish Luther's own thought from that of Melanchthon and Lutheran Orthodoxy, Holl was able to show that Ritschl had not gone far enough in this endeavor. Holl points out elsewhere that it was

4. See Gösta Hök, *Die elliptische Theologie Albrecht Ritschls nach Ursprung und innerem Zusammenhang (Uppsala Universiteits Årsskrift,* 1942, no. 3), esp. pp. 52–137.
5. The most substantial studies of Holl are Otto Wolff, "Die paradoxe Einheit in den Gegensätzen ethizistisch rationalisiert: Karl Holl," *Die Haupttypen der neueren Lutherdeutung* (Stuttgart: W. Kohlhammer, 1938), pp. 318–84; and Walter Bodenstein, *Die Theologie Karl Holls im Spiegel des antiken und reformatorischen Christentums* (Berlin: Walter de Gruyter & Co., 1968). Wolff, like most of Holl's critics, tends to emphasize Holl's debt to Ritschl, while Bodenstein, following Emanuel Hirsch, tends to minimize it. A judicious balance seems to be struck by David W. Lotz, *Ritschl and Luther: A Fresh Perspective on Albrecht Ritschl's Theology in the Light of His Luther Study* (Nashville and New York: Abingdon, 1974), especially the section on "Ritschl and Twentieth-Century Luther Research (Karl Holl)" (pp. 153–61), who sees Ritschl as "an important forerunner" of the Luther-Renaissance and credits Holl with having overcome "the superficiality of the Ritschlian position, namely, Ritschl's failure to comprehend Luther's *theologia crucis.* . . ."

3

Melanchthon who assumed, and taught a whole generation of Lutheran clergymen (if not all of Lutheranism) to assume, that religion necessarily aims at blessedness. But according to Holl, this assumption would give up one of Luther's greatest accomplishments; namely, the consistent elaboration of a religion that teaches one to assume full responsibility for oneself, simultaneously to recognize that all one is and has is God's free gift, and, above all, to participate (in a kind of active passivity or passive activity) in God's transformation of oneself, of others, and of the world itself. It is this basic conception that prompted Holl to look upon Calvin, in Hans Lietzmann's words, as Luther's "only truly congenial disciple."[6]

The dichotomy between religions of blessedness and religions of transformation is reflected in the questions Holl's study purports to answer. What do people look for in religion? Evidently one of two things: a new relationship to themselves, or to the Absolute, God. If people look for the former, their religion is of the "blessedness" type; Feuerbach's analysis of theology as anthropology applies to this type, as do Luther's strictures against "heathen" religion. If people look for the latter type of religion, two further questions present themselves: Is the Absolute (God) knowable, and, is there a duty to know it (or him)? Holl shows that Luther found a positive answer to the second of these questions long before he found one to the first, for indeed the very concept of God, as the Absolute, implies a duty on the part of rational creatures, precisely as relative and creaturely, to relate themselves to him. Of course, the Absolute, as Ideal, must be knowable if its apprehension is to be the motivating force for a religion of transformation. Thus Holl's last question (in this series) reflects even more conclusively than the earlier ones the dichotomy of the two types. Religion can be *either* a vestige of primitivism *or* the motivating force for true progress: the former, insofar as it conforms to the egocentric, quasi-magical, salvation-and-blessedness-for-me type, which creates a god that is really only an extension of the salvation-hungry self; and the latter, in-

---

6. Hans Lietzmann, "Gedächtnisrede auf Karl Holl," *GA* 3, p. 575.

sofar as it apprehends God as the truly Absolute and Ideal—that is, as Love—and allows the person, as part of a growing community, to be transformed into his image and likeness.

But Luther was not so much concerned with a type of religion as with a concrete embodiment of the type, namely, the religion established by Jesus Christ. Taught by Luther, Holl understands Christianity as the unity of three elements: the forgiveness of sins, vouchsafed by God's unmerited love and favor; the higher morality patterned after this divine love or perfection; and the gift of the Holy Spirit or the Christ within, which gradually enables the forgiven sinner to approach closer and closer to meeting the standard until at last, on the Day of Judgment, that standard is actually and fully met. From the divine point of view, this progressive sanctification is wrought entirely and infallibly by God himself; from the human point of view, this progressive sanctification is the life of faith active in love, in community with God and in gratitude for all his gifts, especially for the gift of forgiveness and the promise of conformity with Christ. In principle, the concept of a continuing purgation and sanctification between death and the Judgment is not inconsistent with this understanding of Christianity. What is inconsistent with this understanding, however, is the introduction of the concept of merit, which transforms the blessedness *of* conformity with Christ into blessedness *as the reward for* conformity with Christ, and a "moral" religion of transformation into a "self-seeking" religion of blessedness—while appearing not to do away with Jesus' heightening of the moral demand, the gift of the forgiveness of sins, or the reality of grace, faith, or love.

Holl points out that Augustine and the Scholastics tried to maintain these essential features of Christianity with their conception of "habitual" grace, infused in the soul at the time one's sins are forgiven and enabling one to meet the higher demands of Christian morality. But these higher demands are not *actually* met in this life, of course; they are met only putatively, by imputation or "faith." Protestants sometimes imagine that medieval Catholic theology did not teach the necessity of God's grace and the insufficiency of human efforts to meet the divine requirements

5

apart from that grace. But it did, and in much the same way as Luther (according to Holl): by holding that we are covered by the extrinsic righteousness or merits of Christ until our own intrinsic or actual righteousness is sufficient—as a result of grace—to enable us to stand before God in the Judgment. In the medieval view, however, as Holl points out, all this was thought to operate at a level below the individual consciousness. One's sins were forgiven and supernatural grace infused at baptism, in infancy, before the attainment of consciousness; the supernatural enablement to rise above a merely natural righteousness was thought to operate mysteriously; and insofar as little progress was noted in the quest for full conformity with Christ, purgatory was available to continue and complete the process—once again, beyond the scope of human consciousness in the sense of empirical observation. Augustine's prayer, "Give what Thou commandest, and command what Thou wilt," might be said to reflect this relative indifference to the precise character of the moral goal and the preoccupation with grace as the means to blessedness.

As in his study "Augustins innere Entwicklung" (Augustine's inner development)[7] so here Holl's estimate of Augustine and his influence is perhaps a bit too negative. Luther's discovery that in order to be acceptable to God every deed and every moment of every day must be actually, not merely putatively, "referred" to God, i.e., lived in the consciousness of his presence and in willing subjection to his will, is a distinguishing mark of Catholic Augustinianism. When Holl says that it is here, with Luther's "discovery of the unequivocal greatness of the divine commandment," that "we have the first indications of a reformer in the making," he means to point forward to the eventual break with Catholicism. But in the more ecumenical atmosphere of today, one can hardly overlook the fact that Augustinianism is a recognized "school" within the Catholic tradition.[8] While it is true that Catholic Augustinianism's interpretation of the divine imperative is a minority position, must not the same be said of

---

7. Karl Holl, "Augustins innere Entwicklung," *GA* 3, pp. 54–116.
8. See Eugène Portalié, S.J., "Augustinianisme," *Dictionnaire de Théologie Catholique*, vol. 1, 1902, cols. 2485–501, esp. col. 2489.

Luther's interpretation of that imperative in the Protestant tradition? It would seem to be one of Holl's important achievements to have made this plain.

While Holl elsewhere identifies the uniqueness of the Christian concept of God with God's special interest in the sinner, in the present essay he is concerned to show that Luther's is the *religious* concept of God, as distinct from the philosophical-transcendental and the magical-immanental concepts, which entered the Catholic tradition and led to a dualistic theology and piety: of marvel at God's absoluteness, on the one hand, and of manipulation, on the basis of God's covenant or ordinance, on the other—and in the interest, of course, of one's own blessedness. The religious concept, at the same time, is also the *moral* concept, in the sense that it addresses us as an unconditional "ought"—and promises nothing *in addition to* what it demands, namely, full conformity to Christ, the Ideal. Thus Holl succeeds in overcoming the "elliptical" shape of Christianity as the "perfect moral religion" by showing the coincidence of the two centers or foci—the moral and the religious—pointed up by Ritschl.

The metaphysical basis of this coincidence is a kind of divine determinism called "monergism" (from the Greek *monergein,* "to work alone," as opposed to *synergein,* "to work together, to cooperate," which yields the term "synergism"). W. Bodenstein credits Holl with having coined the term's German equivalent, *Alleinwirksamkeit.*[9] Holl contends that it is largely the monergistic concept of God that sets Luther's personal theology apart from all later "Lutheran" theology. The term denotes the coincidence of God's omnipotence and purposiveness. According to Holl, Luther saw God working everywhere below the threshold of consciousness except in the elect, to whom he appeals through the conscience in order that they may freely respond to his appeal when they recognize the necessity of whatever God asks for the realization of his ultimate goal, the establishment of the perfect community of love. For all created freedom is limited by the absolute freedom of God, which is defined as perception of the

9. Walter Bodenstein, *Die Theologie Karl Holls,* p. 200, n. 30.

7

necessity of God's plan of salvation in terms of his own determinateness as love. Here Luther parts company with the Scotists and Nominalists insofar as they conceived of God as more transcendentally indeterminate. Here, too, Holl parts company with Ritschl, who had been unable to relate such essential Lutheran doctrines as the bondage of the human will, predestination, and divine monergism to the "reformatory" understanding of God as love and had accordingly dismissed them as vestiges of Luther's Ockhamist past.

But if the concept of divine monergism provides Holl's understanding of Luther with its unity, Holl is emphatic in his insistence on the paradoxical character of Luther's religion, the "typically German" ability "to see contradictories in one single vision." For while God works all in all, human beings are nevertheless fully responsible for themselves in the absolute totality of their selfhood. The forgiveness of sins and the promise of total conformity to Christ do not set aside the personal consciousness of sin and judgment. Holl sees Luther following the principle "The greater the responsibility, the more authentic the existence." He accordingly defines religion generally as the "nonabsorptive" union of the human will with God's will, and Luther's personal religion as the existential affirmation of a selfless sense of selfhood.

Holl's presentation appropriately culminates, therefore, in the affirmation of Luther's religion as an active passivity or a passive activity. In prayer, the most arduous work in the world, the believer is nevertheless passive: the purpose of prayer cannot be to change either God's creation or God himself. Rather it is the one who prays who is to be changed, to be brought more fully in line with God's will and to be transformed more and more into the image of Christ. We must learn to submit, rather than try to change what God sends us or substitute something of our own choosing. Yet "as the Father worketh hitherto," so the Christian, too, may take delight in work. But unlike Ritschl, who largely identified the believer's contribution to the kingdom of God with faithful exercise of one's secular vocation, Holl sharply distinguishes these two categories and subordinates one to the other: the Christian's primary responsibility is the spiritual task of advancing the kingdom; fulfillment of one's secular vocation, though important and a divine vocation and responsibility in the full sense of the word, is nevertheless secondary. In a sense, this is a more consistent outworking of Ritschl's subordination of the objective counterpart of the Christian's vocation, namely, the "secular orders," as mere raw material to the ultimate goal of the kingdom of God. Both subordinations were criticized in the 1930s, and Holl was accused of going back, at this point especially, to Ritschl and the nineteenth century.[10]

One of the most significant features of Holl's essay is the stress it places on Luther's *Anfechtungen*—those experiences of seeing his existence before God radically called into question, when God or the devil seemed to be personally assaulting him—as the proof and test of his personal religion. In all of these *Anfechtungen* Luther saw himself faced with the paradoxical requirement to feel morally one with God even while maintaining an attitude of absolute self-condemnation and the sense that it is one and the same person who simultaneously and fully participates both in the righteousness of God and in being condemned as a sinner. But here as elsewhere Holl is not content simply to take note of Luther's paradoxes. He shows how for Luther himself they point toward a synthesis that is both rationally and morally defensible: the rational integrating factor is the concept of divine monergism and the moral integrating factor is the concept of transformation or religious actualization. For Holl's Luther, moreover, these two are really one: for the moral transformation of the believer (i.e., the personal actualization of the moral and religious union with God) is brought about precisely by the God who works— and works alone.

This synthesis combined essential concerns of the two major parties in German Protestantism before World War I: the strong doctrine of God and emphasis on justification pleased the conservatives, and the insistence on religious actualization and personal transformation pleased the liberals. Hans Lietzmann has testified to the effect of Holl's collection of Luther studies along

10. See O. Wolff, *Die Haupttypen der neueren Lutherdeutung*, esp. pp. 382–83.

this line: "When Holl's *Luther* appeared in 1921, it affected us like a sudden, powerful revelation. For our evangelical church, so broken up into factions of all kinds, it was a symbol of victory and unity. Holl succeeded in overcoming much long-standing conflict and awakening once again in many hearts the awareness of the uniform foundation of all our religious and churchly life in the gospel recovered and interpreted by the genius of Martin Luther."[11] But while Holl's scholarship and profound knowledge of Luther were universally recognized, his interpretation of Luther was rejected out of hand by the representatives of the Theology of Crisis school. The spokesman for that school, Friedrich Gogarten, saw in Holl's interpretation of Luther just one more expression of the "scientific theology" of the prewar period which, these theologians contended, was neither scientific nor truly theological.

Gogarten's critique points up three areas in which Holl's Luther-interpretation differs from traditional Lutheranism. The first of these is the area where the doctrine of salvation touches on the doctrine of the person and work of Christ. Gogarten asks, in effect: Who saved Luther—Christ or the First Commandment? Implicit in this question are two criticisms: (1) that Holl assigns only "secondary" importance to Christ, that is, that Holl has an inadequate Christology; and (2) that Holl treats forgiveness as "a rational inference from the fact of the moral consciousness." The first of these charges, especially, has been made again and again against Holl. His response (particularly in notes 28 and 49 below) in the first essay and in "Gogarten's Understanding of Luther," also published here as an appendix, must speak for itself. Holl is presenting Luther's Christology, not his own, and— as a historian—Holl finds that Luther's Christology is both more primitive (i.e., evangelical) and more developed than the traditional Christology taken over by Lutheran Orthodoxy. For Luther, Christ is above all the mediator between God and humanity in the present age, whose function will cease—along with that of the Holy Spirit—in the age to come. What Luther seems to deny is the absoluteness or ultimacy of all mediation, and in

---

11. Adolf von Harnack and Hans Lietzmann, *Karl Holl: Zwei Gedächtnisreden*, p. 4.

this sense it seems appropriate to speak of a *radicalizing of religion* on Luther's part. Luther's personal religion was theocentric not only as over against all egocentric religion but also as over against the Christocentric religion propounded by Ritschl. At this point Holl seems to be more Kantian than Ritschl, for where Ritschl relied on the personal influence of Jesus' life to establish the credibility of the gospel, Holl (or rather, Holl's Luther) relies on the moral law in the sense of Kant's categorical imperative. Holl freely admits that Luther's experience of extreme *Anfechtung*— when Christ himself disappeared from his view and only the First Commandment could save him—*appears* to offer forgiveness *in the form of* a rational inference from the fact of the moral consciousness. But already in the first of Holl's published writings—his review of a book by Friedrich Traub[12]—Holl had noted that all inferences from the categorical imperative (including, specifically, forgiveness) are conditional upon the possibility of its realization in the context of the natural world, and that forgiveness—a primarily religious concept—ought not to be put in the service of a nonreligious (purely ethical or moral) end. Gogarten is right, therefore, in noting a close *formal* similarity between Kantian moralism and Holl's interpretation of Luther. But Gogarten is quite wrong in overlooking the fact that for Holl the ethical or philosophical form, which derives from reflection on the phenomenon of conscience, is merely the form, not the content, of faith. The content of faith is the gospel of God's saving grace, while the demonstration of its moral form is merely a persuasive device, or as Holl puts it, the means of getting from the testimony of the gospel to evangelical conviction.

The second area delimited by Gogarten's critique involves the relationship of justification and sanctification. Holl maintains that, for Luther, justification always includes the entire process of sanctification, and that it is effected by the *Christ within us*. Gogarten's attack on this concept seems to link him to the virulent anti-Pietism which Ritschl shared with Lutheran Orthodoxy. While Holl was no Pietist, he was nevertheless much more able

12. F. Traub, *Die sittliche Weltordnung* (Freiburg i. Br., 1892); Holl's review is in *Göttinger Gelehrte Anzeigen*, 1893, pp. 431–37.

to appreciate the experiential side of religion, and thus to rediscover how Luther had *personalized religion* and morality. The "sentence of justification" is a means to an end for both Holl and Gogarten. But the end is not the same. For Gogarten, as for Melanchthon, the end of justification (i.e., of forgiveness and the imputation of Christ's righteousness) is the blessedness of the individual, irrespective of his moral or religious progress. Morality is understood as response to the law, religion as response to the gospel of Christ's finished work, and both as extrinsic to the believer, whose faith and obedience are accordingly standardized and impersonalized. The damage, from Holl's point of view, is severe: of the three essential constituents of Christianity, only the forgiveness of sins remains; the two aspects of the higher righteousness, namely, its character as taught by the historical Jesus and its being effected within the believer through the indwelling presence of Christ are no longer viewed as essential; to say nothing of the fact that a "moral" religion of transformation has once again been turned into a "selfish" religion of blessedness. For according to Holl and Holl's Luther, the end of justification is the complete sanctification of the forgiven sinner, that is, complete inner transformation into the likeness of Christ, which in itself constitutes blessedness. The paradox is plain: he who seeks to save his life—by whatever means, even by refuge in the cross of Christ—shall lose it, while he who gives it up in order to receive the life of Christ shall receive it back again, transformed in the image of eternity. Luther's religion and morality are inward and personal because they spring from the work of Christ in the soul; and since no two souls are the same, one should expect that the work of Christ in these different souls would lead to different religious and moral results—a divinely fostered pluralism!

The third area of Gogarten's critique of Holl has to do with ethics. Gogarten charges him with having ethicized Luther. Holl's defense is to show that it was Luther himself who *ethicized religion*—not, indeed, in the sense of adding something to religion, but in the sense of getting at the common root of religion and morality in the purposiveness and will of human beings and, ultimately, of God. But while Gogarten thinks here in terms of two unrelated worlds, the absolute world of the gospel of eternal salvation and the purely relative world of everyday life, Holl sees these interrelated as means and end. The everyday world is not merely relative—i.e., irrelevant, from God's point of view—but is and ought to be a means toward the "absolute" end, growth into the likeness of Christ. Holl, to be sure, does not expect to *see* much growth of the world into conformity with Christ—i.e., toward love—but neither does he expect much *visible* progress on the part of the individual Christian. The crucial point is that the goal be recognized, along with the obligation to move toward the goal. Holl recognizes both; Gogarten recognizes neither. For Gogarten the world is and ought to be governed by the unchanging "secular orders" posited in Creation and apparently undamaged by the Fall; there is no functional concept of a kingdom of God that might redeem and perfect the "orders," just as there is no concept of progressive sanctification for the believer. Holl has both. There is a remarkable parallelism, moreover, between Holl's vision of progress—here and now—in the personal and the social sphere: where the believer is linked to Christ, the secular orders are linked to the kingdom of God. Both are provisionally accepted, and both must be brought increasingly into line with the demands of divine love. Holl puts it this way: "Thus the gospel, though it addresses itself directly only to souls, indirectly permeates the secular orders through its concept of love."[13] In Gogarten's thought there is a comparable correspondence, though of opposite tenor: both the believer and the secular orders are accepted as they are "by faith alone," by imputation, without any need for intrinsic change. No wonder Gogarten approves of Karl Barth's designation of ethics as the "great disturbance" (taking the term in a pejorative sense evidently not intended by Barth in his book *The Epistle to the Romans*); for if ethics always revolves around an "ought," such an "ought" indeed signifies "the negation of the present material reality of life," or, in other words, a divine judgment on *what is* in the name of *what ought*

13. Karl Holl, "Der Neubau der Sittlichkeit," *GA* 1, p. 266.

to be. This judgment Holl accepts and Gogarten rejects; and their interpretations of Luther's ethic differ accordingly.[14]

By going back—more effectively than anyone else before him—beyond Lutheran Orthodoxy and Melanchthon to Luther himself, Holl has opened the door to several kinds of dialogue. What we have called Luther's "personalizing" of religion, mainly in connection with the doctrine of justification, should encourage dialogue with Christians of all types: Catholics and Protestants, Calvinists and Wesleyans, conservatives, liberals, and radicals. The "radicalizing" of religion, with its relativizing of all mediation, should open still further doors, namely, to other, non-Christian traditions. The "ethicizing" of religion might well continue and deepen the dialogue with those who regard themselves as modern and secular. "Scientific theology" indeed shows signs of coming back into vogue. As one of its leading representatives, Holl deserves to be better known than through furtive references in recondite footnotes.[15]

WALTER F. BENSE

14. Of interest in connection with the Holl-Gogarten exchange are Ernst Troeltsch's earlier critique of Gogarten, "An Apple from the Tree of Kierkegaard," and "The Debate on the Critical Historical Method: Correspondence Between Adolf von Harnack and Karl Barth," both translated in James M. Robinson, ed., *The Beginnings of Dialectical Theology* (Richmond: John Knox Press, 1968), pp. 311–16 and 165–87. On the latter, which affords some instructive parallels, see H. Martin Rumscheidt, *Revelation and Theology: An Analysis of the Barth-Harnack Correspondence of 1923* (Cambridge: At the University Press, 1972).

15. Prior to the present publication, the following Holl essays have appeared in English translation: *The Distinctive Elements in Christianity* (Edinburgh: T. and T. Clark, 1937; still available from A. Allenson, Naperville, Ill.). *The Cultural Significance of the Reformation* (New York: Meridian Books, 1959); this volume includes an introduction by Wilhelm Pauck, who wrote his doctoral dissertation under Holl and has done much over the last half-century to make Holl known in America. "Martin Luther on Luther," in Jaroslav Pelikan, ed., *Interpreters of Luther: Essays in Honor of Wilhelm Pauck* (Philadelphia: Fortress Press, 1967), pp. 9–34. "The Missionary Methods of the Ancient and the Medieval Church," "The Ecclesiastical Significance of Constantinople in the Middle Ages," "The Religious Foundations of Russian Culture," and "Tolstoy in His Diaries," in *The Unitarian-Universalist Christian* 31, nos. 3–4, 1976, pp. 28ff., 38ff., 45ff., 57ff.; this issue also includes my study, "Eastern Christianity in the Thought of Karl Holl," pp. 5–27. James Luther Adams and/or the undersigned also intend to publish translations of Holl's essays on justification, Calvin and Calvinism, and Luther's social thought—possibly Holl's most significant contribution.

14

What Did Luther Understand by Religion?

Introduction

Four centuries have elapsed since Luther's posting of the Ninety-five Theses ushered in a new era for Christianity. With each recurrence of this anniversary the Protestant church has felt the challenge to analyze itself and compare its present attainments with those of Luther. To date, Protestantism has not produced Luther's superior or even his equal. Despite all his limitations, made evident by four centuries of subsequent life and thought, he far excels our present generation in original creative power. In remembering Luther, we do not memorialize the dead but deal with one who is very much alive and with us.

In taking up the challenge today, it is fairly obvious what must be our point of departure. Scientific, religious, and ecclesiastical developments of the last generation have combined to create a situation that almost forces us to approach Luther from a particular vantage point. Whether or not we regard it as progress, it is obvious that interest in particular religious doctrines has receded in the thought of the present, and religion itself has become the object of our searching and reflection. Philosophy from Kant to Nietzsche, when dealing with spiritual matters, has increasingly conceived its task to be that of elucidating the psychological preconditions. Similarly, the scientific study of history and especially the scientific study of religion, which has made such tremendous strides in the last few years, attempt everywhere to discern the typical, the common essence that reveals itself within the colorful heterogeneity of the religions of the world. The influence of this approach is so strong that it plays a role even in interconfessional discussions within Christianity.

15

Even the peculiar romantic movement toward religion, which almost surprised us by arising among us near the end of the last century, embraced this approach and it has been characterized by a distinct, though usually only sentimental, fondness for the mystical. Here, too, we see the attempt to discard the historical material and the sharply delineated form in order to withdraw into the unmediated, into the realm of pure feeling and intuition. The most pressing religious questions for thinking people today are therefore of a very general kind. What do people really look for in religion? Does religion involve a relationship to an Absolute above and beyond oneself, or is it really only a relationship to oneself, to one's own metaphysical ground of being? Is the Ultimate around which religion revolves hidden from us in impenetrable darkness so that the only possibility is a "silent veneration," a religion of "as if," perhaps even a "religion without God"? Or is it possible for us to approach the deepest mystery, and is there a duty to do so? Is religion, viewed historically, only a carry-over from our most primitive stage, a tenaciously maintained residue of prescientific thinking, or is it something that transcends all mere rationality, the concealed motive force for the whole higher development of humanity?

We do Luther no violence when we try to relate him to these questions. One side of him, it is true, is not at all amenable to this whole approach. For him there was no such thing as "religion in general" or a religion of merely personal experience. He recognized only one true religion, the Christian; and he was able to think of it only as expressed in certain definite statements of faith, transmitted and preserved in a church. Nevertheless, Luther gained his own personal conception of the Christian religion only in a controversy with the Catholic church which forced him to deal with the issues at their most profound level. The meaning of his Reformation is not exhausted in the fact that he changed certain doctrines and institutions of the Catholic church. He rebuilt from the ground up; that is, he began with the concept of God, and eventually touched all the questions that beset us today. We only recognize his uniqueness and depth, therefore, when we accentuate this side of his work.

1. God and His Judgment in Early and Medieval Christianity

What did religion mean to the people of Luther's time? To what extent did the Christianity that was preached actually function as a decisive power in the lives of the people?

From the beginning, Christian piety was based upon the idea of judgment, a verdict that God would one day render concerning the person's worthiness or unworthiness. In its Christian form, this sober faith goes beyond a general sense of responsibility for life as an entrusted blessing that can be enjoyed only once. As articulated by Jesus, it serves as a powerful impulse to raise the standard of self-judgment above the common morality and above a paltry legalism to the height of the divine good. Only that righteousness can endure before God which takes its standard of conduct from the way God himself acts, from his perfection. The concept of God which corresponded to this view was first of all that of the stern judge, which was vigorously affirmed by Jesus himself. Even the last penny must be paid. But to Jesus it was intolerable and contrary to the most obvious facts to picture God only as a disinterested judge who objectively renders his judgment for one side or the other. God actually does not want people to fall into judgment. He wants to save them. He derives more joy from the sinner who returns to him than from the righteous one who has remained with him. He is able to forgive even the worst offenses. Hence the concept of grace, of merciful love, comes to take precedence over retributive justice. Jesus does not thereby annul the idea of judgment. Both the grace and the justice of God are necessary truths for him. This unity in which the three concepts of judgment, moral demand, and faith in the goodness of God are bound together constitutes the power of the Christian religion and an inexhaustible challenge to its theology.

The idea of judgment remained alive in Christianity even when the hope for an early return of Christ disappeared. The church maintained the idea of judgment, crudely to be sure, by using Orphic (and late-Jewish) ideas to transform the pale concept of the intermediate state into that of a purgatory, thereby reminding

17

even the presumably saved believer of a judgment awaiting him immediately after death.   In this form the idea of judgment continued to function through the centuries, goading and disturbing the inner life, arousing doubt regarding the validity of one's own moral performance, serving as a spur to higher effort.   One might say that right up to the present this has been the most striking aspect of the Christian faith as held by the Catholic church.

But even before this conception was fully developed, significant changes in the other critical area, the concept of God, had occurred.   In the age of the apologists, the church borrowed the philosophical concept of God that had already invaded late Judaism: God the Other, ever at rest in himself, the Unapproachable One who far transcends the thoughts and actions of men. The church adopted the concept of God to provide additional support for its concept of the spirituality of God, so important in the struggle with paganism.   At the same time the transcendence of God made an effective contribution to the church's conception of grace: God's mercy seemed to be magnified by reflection on the utter sublimeness of him who deigns to concern himself with human beings.

At the same time another motive exerted an opposite influence. In the Western church the primitive Christian idea of reward evolved into the concept of "merit," into the belief that through extraordinary deeds a certain claim can be made on God.   By coining the technical terms *meritum* and *satisfactio*, Tertullian seemed to give a legal-moral basis to this idea.   But the resulting idea of God conflicted with the first.   The idea of merit implied the kind of God upon whom human beings could exert moral pressure.   But how can human beings with any consistency impose claims upon a God who is supremely and incomparably transcendent, and in the process bring him down to their level? The church was not conscious of the contradiction.   From the time of Tertullian on, it actually became customary to work with two concepts of God: the philosophical concept, to satisfy the rational mind, and the practical concept, to accommodate religious desires.   Inevitably, the authority of the church asserted itself at this point.   Only the fact that the church endorsed the

concept of merits and provided guidance for their acquisition overcame the doubt as to whether one could really approach God
with one's own achievements.

Even Christianity, then, was overcome by the temptation that
besets all religion,[1] the desire somehow to coerce the sublime
power that it venerates. In its entire history, Western theology
was unable to overcome the antithesis between God as he is in
himself and God as he can be moved by human beings. As theology probed more deeply, the antithesis assumed sharper lines.
Scholasticism pursued this antithesis to its ultimate conclusion.
The grand achievement of Scholasticism was that with growing
intellectual power it related all theological questions to the concept of God, and thereby made clear for all time that there is only
one basic theological question, the question of God. In the
process Scholasticism also stressed the point that was of the greatest importance for philosophy: that God must be conceived as
both absolute and personal. But it was never able to regard
absoluteness as anything other than self-sufficient essence. Thomas
Aquinas's whole system is founded upon the view that God is
self-sufficient, that he enjoys his own blessedness by contemplat-
ing himself and his own perfection, and that therefore nothing
outside himself, not even his own creative action, can add to his
satisfaction. Duns Scotus carries this thought even further. He
conceives of God as sovereign will, bound by nothing external or
internal save the law of contradiction. On this basis everything
that God does outside his own being appears as the expression of
a certain royal caprice. God was under no compulsion to create
a world, to put people in it, to redeem them after the Fall, or to
redeem them in the way he has chosen to redeem them. God
owed none of this to them; and he only owed it to himself in the
sense that a great lord is to some extent obliged to be generous.

1. I remind the reader not only of the interconnections between religion and
magic in their beginnings, but especially of a development in late Judaism
that became significant for the development of Catholic Christianity. The
notion that God is the Lord, which was the point of departure of Israelite
religion, was there modified by the notion of covenant, which arose in connection with the growing appreciation of the law. As Lord, God can freely
establish the conditions governing his relationship to human beings. He
does so in his law. But insofar as human beings fulfill the law, they on their
part also have a just claim to be rewarded accordingly.

Human beings could only accept all this as given fact. But the detailed explanation of this fact was supposed to make believers keenly aware of how much God had done for them, even though God did not have to do anything.

Another special proof of God's condescension was seen in his willingness, in view of our sensual nature, to allow his power to work in sensible objects such as sacraments and relics. Nevertheless, Scholasticism was always ready to warn that God was not, strictly speaking, bound by what he had once chosen to do. To be sure, God, in a voluntary act of self-limitation, had established a firm order of creation and redemption, and he himself ordinarily adhered to his moral law. But Duns Scotus and the Nominalists declared that God continues to confront this order in perfect freedom. Occasionally he could break through the natural order with a miracle, as though to show his absolute, lordly power; for a miracle according to Scotus—and here he deviates from Thomas— occurs not only outside nature but also contrary to it. In fact, God had in the past occasionally even disregarded some of the Ten Commandments in his directions to holy men.[2] This power was no mere academic postulate, for miracles were continually being experienced, particularly in connection with the church's activities, and each of them confirmed God's freedom in dealing with nature and people.

On the other hand, the complex of ideas based on the concept of merit was being developed with equal care. Here, too, the Scholastics became aware of the forms and levels of ethical action. Abelard and Bernard of Clairvaux pioneered in distinguishing more sharply between the intention and the external deed, and between the various motives behind the intention.[3] They recognized the difference between a selfishly motivated love of God, a

2. It seems to me that Reinhold Seeberg has underestimated the significance of the *potestas absoluta* in his *Die Theologie des Duns Scotus* (esp. pp. 178–79). The *potestas absoluta* is for Duns not merely a "hypothetical" supposition; it is actualized again and again next to the *potestas ordinata*. It is surely no accident that Seeberg nowhere, as far as I can see, deals with Scotus' conception of miracles. The moral order was breached in three cases that are thoroughly discussed by Duns: God's command to Abraham to sacrifice Isaac, the theft of the vessels of the Egyptians, and the demand that Hosea should marry a harlot.

3. The origins of these distinctions are to be found in Aristotle and the Stoics, but the contribution of monasticism and penitential instruction must not be forgotten.

merely grateful love, and a love of God for his own sake. But ultimately this refinement of moral perception only promoted the further development of the idea of merit. While the very concept of merit postulated a distance between obligatory and supererogatory works, between things that God strictly commands and others that he only "counsels," it now became possible to bridge this distance with a hierarchy of moral actions. For morality itself, however, everything depended upon the location of the lower limit, the measure of what is barely sufficient and obligatory in the strictest sense.

It was fateful for the Middle Ages that Augustine not only had introduced the concept of a "lesser righteousness adequate for this life" but also had taken self-love for granted and recognized it as a legitimate motive for action. Following him, the Scholastics reduced the minimum required by the basic Christian commandment to love God and the neighbor to a level where personal comfort and advantage would not be seriously jeopardized. Every action demanding considerable self-control was therefore valued as an evidence of heroic perfection. Loving God with the whole heart and the whole soul was the supreme achievement whose attainment, though indeed fervently desired in this earthly life, could not be absolutely required of anyone. The influence of Aristotle gave sanction to the Scholastics of the High Middle Ages to lower the standards even more. In their analyses of "natural morality," the Scholastics felt constrained not only to recognize a morality outside Christianity, but even to concede to such philosophical standards a certain validity within Christianity. Actions considered good from a philosophical point of view—that is, actions corresponding to our rational nature—had to be regarded as at least neutral even from a Christian point of view. Sin, in its full sense, began only with a violation of the natural moral law. Thus a long ladder stretched from the barely permissible to the most perfect and meritorious, and the believer was free to choose how high he wanted to climb. The most practically important implication, however, was that the greater merit exerted stronger pressure on God, who was expected to reward it, and thus constituted a just claim to a higher degree of blessedness.

To be sure, the Schoolmen tried hard to harmonize these

21

radically divergent trains of thought. Every celebration of the Mass impressively proclaimed that people depend upon grace, for the Mass was intimately connected with the fundamental act of grace, the sacrifice on the cross, and constituted its continually efficacious renewal. But in extolling the boundless mercy of the Son of God who daily permits himself to be sacrificed anew upon the altars of Christendom, one also felt constrained to exalt the power that is granted to the priest, that is, to a human being. The Middle Ages coined the coarse expression *"conficere deum"* for what the priest effects in transubstantiation: the priest "makes God." This was as intoxicating an idea as that of the divine presence.[4]

The result was the same when, following Augustine, the attempt was made to limit the concept of merit by representing God as the dispenser of the power to do meritorious deeds. According to the Scholastic elaboration of Augustine's conception, the sacrament was said to "infuse" a supernatural power, a new *habitus,* the supernatural love of God, by whose cooperation alone the good deed becomes meritorious, that is, worthy of eternal life (see

---

4. Even today this is a favorite subject for first sermons by students for the priesthood. Compare also the 1905 pastoral letter of Archbishop Katschthaler of Salzburg, which expresses the prevalent views: "Where even in heaven is there power like that of the Catholic priest? With the angels? With the Mother of God? Mary conceived Christ, the Son of God, in her womb and gave birth to him in the stable at Bethlehem. Indeed; but consider what occurs in holy Mass. Does not the same thing, in a way, take place under the consecrating hands of the priest in this sacred act? Under the forms of bread and wine, Christ becomes truly, actually, and essentially present and is born again, as it were. . . . Mary once brought the holy Child into the world. But lo, the priest does this not once but hundreds and thousands of times, as often as he celebrates Mass. There in the stable the holy Child that was given to the world through Mary was small, susceptible to suffering and death. Here on the altar, under the hands of the priest, it is Christ in his majesty, immune to suffering and death, as he sits in heaven at the right hand of the Father, gloriously triumphant, perfect in every respect. He has put the priests in his place to continue the same sacrifice which he offered. He has given them authority over his holy humanity, power over his own body, as it were. The Catholic priest is not only able to bring about his presence on the altar, shut him up in the tabernacle, distribute him for the benefit of believers; he can even present him, the incarnate Son of God, as a sacrifice for the living and the dead. Christ the only-begotten Son of God the Father, through whom heaven and earth were created, who sustains the whole universe, submits here to the will of the Catholic priest." (Carl Mirbt, *Quellen zur Geschichte des Papsttums,* 3d ed., p. 401.) Catholic dogmaticians are always at great pains to find expressions that disguise the magical element in this whole conception.

Rom. 5:8). By designating this imparted grace as a *habitus*, the Schoolmen intended to elucidate it psychologically, and at the same time to establish its reality. The expression was connected with the Aristotelian teaching of the *hexeis*, the enduring fixities of the soul which are acquired through practice and which imply readiness to act in a certain direction. It was emphasized, however, that in this case the *habitus* was not acquired but miraculously infused through the supernatural working of the sacrament. Nevertheless, it was thought to operate somewhat like a natural *habitus*, inasmuch as abilities and powers, though now of a supernatural sort, result from it.

On this basis, one could develop an outlook like Paul's which referred every good deed back to grace. Thomas made a serious start in this direction. But this view, which ascribed everything to God, was not the only valid one, much less the one that set the standard for the actual attitude of believers. Moreover, even Thomas retained as complementary a view that reemphasized the concept of merit within the *habitus* doctrine. This doctrine stressed what was still required of a person. Through the grant of the *habitus*, one was "justified" before God. Yet that did not mean that everything was settled between oneself and God or that one was sure of eternal life. One was merely lifted above oneself, transplanted to a higher level where one was now acceptable to God. But one was still confronted by the task of producing, by means of these newly acquired supernatural abilities, the merits that would actually open the gate of heaven. The *habitus* was not to be regarded as a magical power on which one could rely. It provided a stimulus, so to speak, toward the good, but it did not operate in a coercive fashion. Therefore the church constantly admonished people to "awaken" acts of love to God on the basis of the *habitus*, that is, to raise the infused love for God to the level of conscious feeling. Only thus would the *habitus* become dynamically operative. But then the theologians again posed the legitimate question, whether in this cooperation the *habitus* or human free will was the ultimately decisive factor. Duns Scotus, with his usual acumen, demonstrated against Thomas that the will, since it determines the objective, is actually decisive, while the impersonal *habitus* is simply a means. But Scotus penetrated even more deeply into the relationship between these two factors. The Franciscan school had always opposed the idea that God, so to speak, simply imposes habitual grace upon people. That would contradict both the uniformity of God's activity and human freedom. In one way or another, people had to prove in advance that they were fit for this new level of life. If they could not immediately attain to the highest achievements, they could at least do something; they could "do what was in them." But where there was achievement, there was also merit—not merit in the fullest sense, but at least a merit corresponding to the human effort involved *(meritum de congruo)*.

The liberality that is appropriate to one in a high place required that God should not overlook this modest but well-intentioned effort on the part of a person.[5] But this transformed the whole conception into its opposite. Even though it was continually asserted that, strictly speaking, habitual grace was not "merited," and even though Scotus might strongly insist that it remained God's prerogative to decide how highly he would value merit, it was still true that a person could extort something even from a sovereign God. Congruent merit was the fine thread by which one could draw everything else, eventually even habitual grace, to oneself.

2. Late-Medieval Piety, German Mysticism, Renaissance Humanism

Corresponding to the dichotomy within the concept of God, piety was also split in two parts. On the one hand, religion was the glorification of God, a sense of astonishment at that power which could so freely govern all things and which still proved to be so generous in dealing with human beings. The greater the astonish-

5. See my essay, "Die iustitia dei in der vorlutherischen Bibelauslegung des Abendlandes" [The righteousness of God in the biblical interpretation of the West before Luther], in *GA* 3, pp. 171ff.

ment, the more credible became its object. The awe inspired by the unpredictable only increased the rapture of the feeling. The extravagant praise of the sacrament of the altar, the coarse features attributed to the saints, the increasing crudity of the legends, the degeneration of the religious plays, the oddness of the relics that were being made available, the multiplication of pilgrimages and shrines, the bizarre miracles that were reported everywhere, and the fabulous element in preaching, all bear witness to the powerful attraction the incredible and the excessive exerted upon people's minds. The full scorn of the "enlightened" could not prevail against this desire to see and experience the supernatural in the miraculous. At the same time all the delight of the waning Middle Ages in play, feast, and color, as well as the ambition of princes, civic pride, and competition among the smaller guilds and brotherhoods, contributed to this type of worship, so strongly, in fact, that there is some doubt whether the religious or the secular element predominated. Piety became loud and impetuous, excitable and ostentatious. Piety tended toward outer show and appealed strongly to mass emotion.

The other half of religion was an equally fervent attempt to attain the standard necessary for entrance into heaven through merits, confessions, indulgences, masses, pilgrimages, and endowments. The *summae confessorum,* which were being written in increasing number since the thirteenth century, correlated all the relationships of everyday life and the problems of an advancing economic life with the church's scale of morality. The laity thus became more dependent on the priests who counseled them. But they did not mind this. They gladly delegated the responsibility for their acts to the priest, for the finer distinctions between individual cases were now increasingly intended to ease the conscience rather than to arouse in it a holy disquiet. Even where personal earnestness roused itself, the stress was much more likely to be on training "virtuosos of the confessional"[6] than on the enhancing of moral power. The moral effect of religion was undoubtedly declining rapidly. While marveling at the magnificent churches

6. This expression was coined by Luther: *artistae illi confitendi* (*WA* 6, p. 166, l. 28).

and the superb town halls of the time, we must not forget to cast a glance into the back alleys. What was found there, even in the very smallest towns, also belonged to the "culture" of the declining Middle Ages.

But behind these two aspects of piety stood the painful question: Where do the two meet? Where does the grace that descends from God meet the human striving that is trying to approach God, in such a way that the individual becomes absolutely sure of God? There were high points at which one might seem to approach this assurance—when, as part of an enraptured crowd, one was lifted beyond oneself, or when, in the sacrament of penance or the Eucharist, one almost palpably experienced the power and mercy of God with the help of the church. But there was no lingering on these mountaintops. Doubts immediately arose in the mind of the brooder: perhaps this experience had been an overflow of emotion; would God require more at the judgment than had been accomplished thus far? This is the reason such piety has to exert itself in ever new beginnings that start first from one side and then from the other.

Now if the individual experienced love for God only sporadically, the same could be said of the crowd. The popularity of the *danse macabre* in art and the great success that Savonarola enjoyed in his early years on account of his preaching of repentance show how eager people were to expose themselves to repeated goading. To be sure, the sudden reversal in Florence also reveals the other side—that this eagerness quickly exhausted itself in one strong outburst.

The church actually desired to maintain the residue of doubt which always remained in this relationship to God. This residue was regarded as pedagogically wholesome. Therefore the church constantly worked in both directions. It frightened people with pictures of purgatory and hell, only to console them immediately with extravagantly dispensed indulgences. While making it easy for the masses, the church stimulated spiritual ambition to ever new meritorious deeds, and readily forgave the worst of sinners. But what was actually accomplished was the validation of the natural hunger for life, the desire for a complete and never-ending happiness, as the strongest motive for religion. The church relied on this motive when it extolled God as the highest good, as the object of a unique enjoyment: but it also appealed to it when purgatory and hell were held up before the eyes of the coarser element.

Since the fourteenth century two movements, each following its own unique course, were competing with this popular religion. The first was that of the German mystics, who were disgusted by the noise and externality that prevailed. They had discovered that the restless concern for good works, the conforming of oneself to other people's standards, and the regular interrogations of the father-confessor only militated against the real goal of religion, the union with God. They identified the most serious flaw in the piety of the church when they opposed the desire for reward and the selfish quest for blessedness as the worst enemies of true love for God. God must be found in the inner self, they thought, and he can be found there only at the price of purging oneself of all unclean desires.

These mystics, then, returned to the old philosophic concept of God as the One, wholly transcendent, completely simple, without name; they claimed that this concept was the only valid one. With this claim they combined the conviction that this distant God is nonetheless immediately present in the ground of every human soul. The latter element is most characteristic. Faith in the divine spark had already been affirmed in Neoplatonic mysticism, which no doubt exercised an influence here, and the way for it had been prepared by previous developments within Scholasticism (the *syntheresis* as the *scintilla*) and mysticism (as in the school of Saint Victor). But the breakthrough of this point of view in the personal self-awareness was something new. It was obviously connected with the general enhancement of self-awareness which had followed the economic and political advances. German mysticism reflects the same atmosphere as the theology of Duns Scotus and the originators of the Renaissance.

German mysticism sharply opposed this sense of personality, however, insofar as it was purely secular. The mystics' conception of God, faith in the One that embraces all and that alone is real, could not allow anything else in the world to regard itself as existing somehow apart and for itself. Its particular historical situation led German mysticism to approach the union with God in a new way. The real barrier to a return to God was not individuation as such, but selfhood, self-will, "self-acceptation."

Correspondingly, the mystics also changed their conception of the way that leads to God. Unlike the earlier mystics, they demanded not only the mortification of the inclination toward the creaturely, the sensual, the distracting; they also insisted especially on the destruction of the consciousness of the ego as something that stands over against God. To this end they required willing assent to whatever afflicts and distresses one's self-consciousness— to suffering, misfortune, ill repute; they went so far as to demand that the individual should feel unworthy even of suffering and punishment. Through such self-discipline, people were to become resigned to God's will and free from the desire for reward, the selfish striving for beatitude, and the impatient longing for redemption. But once they had attained such complete quietude of the will, the restoration of the original unity with God would follow as a matter of course. For after the process of "unbecoming" (*entwerden*) had been completed, the "nameless" self cleaves to the nameless divinity; and then God, if he be a just God, must fill the person; the hour must come when the "Son of God is born within" the one who, drunk with salvation, sinks into the sea of the Godhead.

German mysticism performed the great historical service of first sharply formulating the question that is crucial for all personal religion, namely, whether a sense of God and a pronounced sense of self are compatible. But even measured by their own standards, the mystics did not completely answer the questions they raised. That they did not achieve a stable God-consciousness, however, is not a charge that can be made especially against them. For them, as for all mystics, times of quickening were necessarily followed by disenchantment, aridity, remoteness from God, temptation (*Anfechtung*), and the torments of hell. In the very same moment in which contact with God was achieved, separation would begin to occur. But a deficiency characteristic of German mysticism appears in this, that it imparted new strength to the very enemies it attacked most resolutely. It fought against eudaemonism in religion but ended up by intensifying it to the highest degree. A subtle epicureanism permeated its whole quest, even more than it did the churchly piety. The mystics ostensibly renounced all happiness; they wanted only God himself, not his gifts; but they made this renunciation of the earthly only with the ulterior motive of saving themselves for the choicest delights. In anticipation of these, pain itself was regarded as a delight. In someone like Suso, this leads to a genuine masochistic passion; the fact that he cannot consistently remain on the mountaintop becomes a secret source of pleasure, for it makes possible a new striving, a new aspiration that is almost sweeter than the goal itself.

German mysticism, furthermore, preached extermination of selfhood, and yet was not able to keep the self from strongly asserting itself, from self-seeking. Every mystic wants solitude and needs it. In German mysticism we find the additional desire not to be disturbed by anyone else in one's self-development. Tauler even suggests that to find God one ought to cease to take pleasure in other "Friends of God" and other good men. Yet when the goal has been achieved, the mystic's sense of selfhood simply will not disappear. Supposedly having been engulfed in the sea of the Godhead, one cannot help sensing that one has achieved the ultimate, and that no one else has experienced it in quite the same way. Why do the mystics speak as they do? Is it because they feel privileged in their temptations and wonderful experiences that they like to speak so much about them, though under the guise of reporting the experiences of others—others who have progressed further than they?

In similar manner the German mystics ended up holding inconsistent attitudes toward evil and guilt. They deepened the sense of sin; they even regarded "venial" sins with due seriousness; they opposed the Brothers of the Free Spirit who believed they had risen above sin. But because of their own concept of God the temptation remained to regard sin as merely adverse experience, and to extend their calm acceptance of all adversity to sin itself. Tauler once gave the advice to let sin pass by on the other side, and not to torment oneself by thinking of it, since it really has nothing to do with the inner being.

The Renaissance also attempted to simplify piety, but in an entirely different mood. The "Renaissance" in a proper sense—for in its broader aspect it permeates the entire medieval period— denotes that specific historical moment in which the secular feeling of selfhood already referred to is formed into an ideal and becomes the prototype of the power-conscious personality that knows how to master and mold the world, showing what it means to be truly human by raising all of its activity to the level of art. Implied in this was the affirmation of economic, political, and intellectual life as independent values, as activities that fully satisfy and that elevate human dignity. From this view issued a cool or negative attitude toward religion and the church. From the middle of the fifteenth century, however, a change began to take place, at least in certain quarters. The question arose whether the "mundane" does in fact satisfy or whether religion is not also a part of the cultivation of a full humanity. This did not mean, however, that such people were about to return unconditionally to the church and Christianity. They clung to what they had previously prized, especially because they found strong stimuli toward religion within antiquity itself, even prior to Christianity and the church. In Cicero and Seneca they discovered a belief in providence and an ethic that was extraordinarily close to that of the gospels. Edification derived from Saint Paul could be matched by a similar faith in redemption in Plato and in the mysticism of Dionysius the Areopagite. The non-Christian sources seemed to have the advantage of being derived directly from the universally human.

A reconciliation was attempted through the reinterpretation of Christianity in universally human terms. Here we find the origin of that general concept of religion[7] which received its greatest development in the Enlightenment. This reinterpretation not only deprived the traditional "paganism" of its meaning, but in reference to Christianity itself, established a point of view with far-reaching implications. The comparison of Christianity with the

---

7. Zwingli dealt with the contrast between Catholicism and Protestantism by writing *On True and False Religion*.

religion of antiquity led the Renaissance humanists to inquire what was really essential in Christianity—the quest for the "essence of Christianity" originates here. Were the essential elements those stressed by the church, or were they the ones that possess universal human appeal? In order to answer this question the Renaissance reached back to the sources, the New Testament and the church fathers, and thereby achieved incisive results. Scholastic theology was rejected as ingenious sophistry. The value of the many ceremonies and of the hierarchy for the promotion of faith and love was questioned. The similarity between the veneration of the saints and the ancient veneration of the gods was pointed out, and even basic doctrines of the church such as that of the Trinity were not beyond criticism. But humanism labored under the disadvantage of being an exclusively academic movement. Its representatives never had the intention of helping the common people to advance. Moreover, they were always inwardly handicapped by the unwillingness of the intellectual to conclude his research and to express his inward thoughts freely to others. Consequently humanism lacked creativity. The Renaissance undermined everything; but it did not convulse people's souls, and it poured no new fire into them.

The tension between these progressive movements and churchly piety at the beginning of the sixteenth century was no longer very severe. The differences never went beyond a certain point. None of the advocates of reform sought a rupture with the church or with Catholic Christianity. Eckhart submitted himself to the church, and his followers were even more careful to maintain their solidarity with it. They recommended its means of grace, especially the sacrament of the altar (used in its proper spiritual sense), as the best means for inner strength and enlightenment. Erasmus did not think he was born to be a martyr, and this disposition was imparted to those who were inspired by him. If we view the century before Luther as a whole, it is significant that the most diverse movements gradually blended with each other and thereby lost some of their uniqueness. Even in Tauler, one is amazed to encounter in the midst of Pauline and Augustinian thought-patterns formulas like "doing what is in you," or to see the Tauler who preaches complete indifference to all suffering and even to hell suddenly give recognition to purgatory. Conversely, Nominalistic theologians like Gerson and D'Ailly were then the most widely read representatives of mysticism. Just as the representatives of the Renaissance, conscious of their own religious weakness, finally clung to the church and in some degree even tried to defend it, so strictly scholastic theologians like Cajetan participated fully in humanistic endeavors. Matters were not heading for a break but toward compromise, toward a synthesis, as we would say today. There may have been an upper stratum that shared a simpler and more informed piety; but the religious ceremonies seemed indispensable for the masses.

It is wrong to think that the generation before Luther was in a passionate inner turmoil, impatiently searching for a deeper religious basis of life.[8] The times were far too prosperous for that, and too much concerned with political, economic, scholarly, artistic, and generally intellectual problems. The religious question was only a part of their problem, and we may doubt that it was the most important one. Certainly, there was an immense amount of sighing and complaining about the church; it was even reviled and ridiculed. What was lacking was the holy wrath that gives vent to an outraged religious consciousness. For in spite of all the criticism that was leveled against it, no one felt very uncomfortable within the church.

3. Luther's Religious Development

Luther's beginnings were marked by an ingenuous devotion to the piety of the church. When he became concerned about his soul's salvation, he chose the way provided by the church for the serious-minded—he entered the monastery. He was not catapulted into

8. See the classic work of G. von Below, *Die Ursachen der Reformation, Historische Bibliothek,* vol. 38 (1917), where all the factors working for and against a reformation are carefully compared and evaluated.

the monastery merely through the accident of an external event.[9] Though there had been no previous inner breakdown, we learn from hints given by Luther himself that within the happy, active comrade (as Mathesius describes him) there was a certain tendency toward melancholy and dissatisfaction with the prevailing spirit of piety. The vow made in sudden fear was probably also a liberation for him, the fulfilling of a secret desire.

To enter the cloister meant to take with utter seriousness the task that confronted every Catholic Christian. There was good reason why monasticism was known as both the estate of penitence and the estate of perfection.[10] The incentives governing churchly morality were here developed to the highest degree. The monastic discipline was designed first of all to transform the sense of one's own unworthiness before God into the strongest possible conviction. Its various regulations trained the individual to engage in the strictest self-examination and to think even of small failures as coming under the divine scrutiny. But over against the deep sense of contrition which grew out of this experience there were for the monk equally strong counterinfluences. At his disposal were not only the comfort which the church offered every believer, especially in the sacrament of penance; an inner strength also came

9. Hans G. von Schubert (*Luthers Frühentwicklung* [1916], p. 13, n. 2) has corrected a misleading earlier remark of Otto Scheel (see *Martin Luther* [3d ed.], vol. 1, p. 322, n. 54): the expression "apparition," with which Luther's father later reproached him, should not be interpreted as a real "vision" which Luther would claim to have had. His own understanding of "apparition" is clearly shown by his own usage (*WA* 7, p. 665, l. 9; 15, p. 688, l. 26; 26, p. 153, l. 35; 30², p. 296, l. 10) where it always means deception or illusion. . . . The "call" Luther thought he heard from heaven likewise consisted merely of the fear evoked by the lightning: ". . . and I believed myself called from heaven by the terrors (*terroribus*) . . ." (*WA* 8, p. 573, l. 31). A vision is unlikely for the reason that Luther never was susceptible to that sort of thing. But how lightning could affect him in a certain state of mind is shown in *WA* 5, p. 354, l. 14, where Luther writes that those cast down in their conscience "dread anything pertaining to lightning and are terrified by the sound of a falling leaf."

10. To the question raised by Heinrich Denifle (*Luther und Lutherthum*, 2d ed. [1904], vol. 1, pp. 133ff.) about the meaning of this expression, I shall return in "Der Neubau der Sittlichkeit" [The reconstruction of morality]. Here it is sufficient to emphasize that the monk who has entered an order has already become (in spite of Denifle) more "perfect" than the layman. He has made a vow that signifies the sacrifice of his whole life to God, and thereby he has already acquired exceptionally high merit.

33

to him from special sources. The very fact that he was a member of a religious order gave strong support to his religious self-awareness. The vow itself was valued as extraordinarily meritorious. Moreover, the monk was in a position to fulfill the Christian's supreme obligation—wholehearted love to God—more freely and therefore more perfectly than the person living in the world, and thereby was able to enhance his position before God. Eventually, even the feeling of unworthiness before God, which he was dutifully cultivating in himself, could be turned directly into a feeling of exultation. The humility he derived from the consciousness of his sin was precisely the attitude that recommended him to God.[11]

Despite the high tension between contradictory feelings, a certain balance was achieved. But complete certainty concerning one's personal relationship to God was not supposed to be attained even in this estate. Yet as long as both feelings, contrition and inner satisfaction, were present and balanced each other, one's condition was easily bearable. One merely had to avoid going to extremes in either direction. The sense of sin ought not to rob a person of comfort so as to drive him to despair; and inner peace ought not to become presumption. The latter was seen as the greater danger; the former was the anxiety of the "overly scrupulous."

According to Luther's own testimony, there was a time when this kind of piety sufficed him. But this could not have been for long. The experience that led him into the monastery had provided an impulse that prevented his becoming really content with himself. The fear of death, in which he had made his vow, affected him so deeply because it was associated with fear of the divine judgment.[12] This concept, which had furnished the original

11. Because of the relationship to Luther, I lay special stress on the emphasis given by Gerson to this idea in his *De consolatione theologiae*. Here is one of the points where Luther differs from Gerson.

12. The difference between Luther and, say, Tolstoy becomes evident here at the very outset. While Tolstoy's inner deepening was brought on by the notion of death as such, that is, by the ultimately purely physical revulsion against annihilation, in Luther's case the impetus was provided by the remembrance of his future accountability for something required of him. This difference directly explains the different conclusions Luther arrived at

motive, remained at the center of his thinking. It is the key to his whole inner development.

From the outset Luther grasped the concept of judgment in a deeper, purer, and more personal sense than was customary among his contemporaries. The sensual conceptions with which Catholicism had surrounded it seem to have dropped away immediately. There is no evidence that the idea of physical punishments that might await him either in purgatory or hell ever made any impression on him. What distressed him was the very concept of judgment itself, the idea of accounting to God. But in this inescapable judgment, the prospect of rendering his account *by himself* bothered him most of all. No matter how many people counseled and helped him here—and he always acknowledged their help gratefully—no one would be with him at the Last Judgment. There he would be totally on his own. This conception gripped him as realistically as if it were a present reality. It was necessary, he felt, to prepare now for this ultimate confrontation. The idea of judgment gave rise to a strong sense of personal accountability, of total responsibility for himself, his beliefs, his way of life. With judgment already present, he felt constrained to come fully to terms with it here and now. The consciousness that he must bear final responsibility, and therefore also desires to bear it, and the need to attain full clarity concerning his relationship to God, his "justification" or reprobation: these are the insights that elevated him above his contemporaries and forced him from the outset to go his own way in opposition to a church that favored the evasion of responsibility and emphasized the uncertainty of God's verdict. Very early, even before 1509, this tendency can be seen in Luther.

Soon, however, he encountered a second, equally powerful stimulus that was also connected with the idea of judgment. The account he was to render to the Supreme Judge not only awakened in Luther a vague dread and increased zeal for good works which others also experienced, but it forced him—and here he exhibits

---

concerning both the relationship to God and ethics. See my essay "Tolstoi nach seinen Tagebüchern, *GA* 2, pp. 433–49 ("Tolstoy and His Diaries," *Unitarian-Universalist Christian* 31, nos. 3–4, 1976, pp. 57–69).

his more perceptive nature—to independent reflection on the meaning of the divine demand. As soon as he saw God himself behind the divine command as giving it and requiring the account, the command acquired new weight. It now became the proclamation of an inflexible will that would brook no deviation or diminution. Impressed by this, he began to see clearly that the goal of his monastic efforts, love to God with his whole heart and soul, was not, as he had previously believed, merely a desirable ideal that one should strive after, but an unconditional duty to be fulfilled completely at every moment. God always requires a total, undivided response. Nothing short of perfection satisfies him. It must be thus, if God is really the Holy One. Nothing impure, nothing defiled by the presence of ulterior motives, may ever be allowed in his presence. Does God, the Giver of all good, not have the right to expect that we love him with our whole soul? Is it not self-evident that the will that turns to him must be a joyful one issuing from the innermost impulses of one's being? Otherwise, all service of God is insincere, a mere sham.

By virtue of this insight, the gradations in morality which the church had made lost all value for Luther. He no longer regarded anything that fell short of perfection, whether it was so-called servile fear or selfishly oriented love of God, as a merely human and therefore excusable imperfection, or as a promising start toward better things. Rather, it was sin, the very opposite of what God desires.

With this discovery of the unequivocal greatness of the divine commandment we have the first indications of a reformer in the making. Without knowing it, Luther was reversing the whole development that had begun in the second century with the elaboration of a double morality. His conscience had now become different from that of his Catholic environment. There some freedom of movement and a mild indulgence in moral matters were deemed proper; for him, morality was immutable. Catholicism started with human ability in its effort to determine what might be attained; Luther started with God, whose honor requires absolute insistence upon his will. Thus Luther's feeling of guilt was also changed. What tormented him was not that his deeds

36

resulted in separation from God, that is, in the loss of a good, but that the fact of the offense appeared to him as something that could never be rectified.[13]

This is why Luther's new perception produced in him a great inner upheaval. Unlike most novices, his "monastic struggles"[14] were not directed against the temptation to return to the life of the world. We find no evidence that the cowl, once assumed, was oppressive to him. We may properly take his word for it that sensuality hardly troubled him.[15] His inner struggles were not primarily defensive at all; on the contrary, they were efforts toward positive achievement. For him, everything depended on attaining that perfect love which God required of him. What was something of a game even within mysticism—for where there is no inflexible duty all striving is a mere game—became for him something holy, something utterly serious.

But when he really faced this task, he found it not only difficult but actually impossible. He never arrived at the point where he could claim in good conscience that a harmony of his will with God's had been attained. This seemed to be easy for others. Later on he confessed that Bonaventure made him quite frantic with his description of the soul's union with God. He always remained in doubt whether the will he had presented to God had

13. This attitude separates Luther from all those who influenced his development. Luther's inner struggles take place on a much higher plane than any of them attained. What he borrows from them—and gratefully—he always interprets in a different sense. . . .

14. Otto Scheel has described these struggles as Luther's coming to grips with the Catholic view of God's retributive justice (and with the doctrine of predestination). No doubt this is an important factor, but it is still secondary. The idea of retribution begins to torment Luther only when he sees himself confronted by requirements he is absolutely unable to meet. I think it is necessary today to emphasize that Luther's solution of this problem did not do away with God's retributive justice. He continues to recognize its validity, along with the idea of judgment. "Die Rechtfertigungslehre in Luthers Vorlesung über den Römerbrief mit besonderer Rücksicht auf die Frage der Heilsgewissheit" [The doctrine of justification in Luther's Lectures on Romans, with special attention to the question of assurance of salvation] in *GA* 1, pp. 111–54 and the essay cited in n. 5 above.

15. *WA*, TR 1, p. 47, ll. 15ff. . . . Denifle's opposite assertion rests upon a wrong interpretation of Luther's concept of concupiscence. See *GA* 1, pp. 111–54, and Luther's own explanation, *WA* 40², p. 92, ll. 1 ff.: "When I was a monk I considered myself damned whenever I felt the concupiscence of the flesh, *as a bad emotion, being displeased with a brother*; and the flesh would conclude: 'you are in sin.'"

really been perfect and pure. He experienced this anguish in prayer, at the altar,[16] and especially when, in line with the church's directives, he deliberately produced an "act of love to God" or a "good intention." An act that had to be deliberately planned, a deliberate resolve to call forth a certain frame of mind, is by that very fact not the constant will that God requires. The best that can be said for it is that it does for a moment what God requires us to do without ceasing. More than that, deliberately to call forth an act means overcoming a resistance to it; it means overcoming an aversion to duty. Luther was honest enough to confess this. But was not this inner opposition to God real sin, serious sin? Even when it was possible instantly to shake off this inertia, was the resulting love of God really genuine? Did not a little self-deception always creep in? Did not the fact that it was forced make it insincere, even hypocritical? In any case, it was not the free, joyful turning to God with the whole heart which Luther felt obliged to render. He faced an insoluble problem. He knew that he should seek God in love, and he desired this as earnestly as anyone. But as soon as he exerted himself he discovered that at the very outset the exertion itself invalidated the act. This was the noose in which he was caught and which threatened to strangle him.

In this situation the remedies the church offered were of no help. Remembering the *habitus,* the supernatural powers supposedly infused in the soul in the sacrament of baptism, did not help at all. Where could he find evidence that this mysterious power motivated him inwardly and mediated to him a supernatural ability? All he could perceive was his own hopeless desire. Even the sacrament of penance was no help to him. Luther diligently utilized it, as did all those who found themselves in this situation. He confessed daily, he confessed even the smallest things, he even confessed the past over and over again. But the result was not what he hoped for. If he felt elevated for the moment through absolu-

---

16. *EA* 9, p. 291: "I also wanted to be a holy, pious monk, and prepared myself for the Mass and prayers with great devotion. But when I was most devout I went to the altar a skeptic and returned from the altar a skeptic. Even when I had made my confession I doubted. When I had omitted it I despaired. For we were under the delusion that we could not pray and would not be heard unless we were as pure and sinless as the saints in heaven."

tion or through the private Mass, the aftertaste was all the more bitter for him. He believed, as directed by the doctrine of the church, that a new power of grace had been poured into him which could continually raise him above himself, and he was crushed when he found that he was basically the same man as before. When, to relieve the situation, he tried more scrupulously to fulfill the conditions requisite for obtaining the blessing of this means of grace, he was all the more thrust into difficulties. The very distinction between mortal and venial sins, so important for Penance, caused him torment. Where really was the boundary? The neat distinctions of the theologians looked good on paper: mortal sin terminated the love of God, while venial sin only disturbed it. But who was able to apply this distinction in a particular situation? Does one ever view oneself so objectively as to be able to say precisely what one's motives are in individual cases? Even more painful for him was the condition for forgiveness. The contrite soul was to receive it. But according to the theologians, contrition—Luther never granted the validity of attrition, based on fear[17]—springs from the love of God. So Luther was back at his starting point. He was traveling in a circle, unable to find his way out.

It would be a superficial judgment to regard Luther as overly scrupulous because of these grave misgivings. If he had been scrupulous in the casuistic sense, he would never have found the way out of his plight. A scrupulous person is one who never finds peace because the will to find it is absent; the disquiet is actually a source of enjoyment, every new doubt furnishes secret pleasure. Luther was of a different temperament. He earnestly wanted to put an end to his misgivings because he felt that he ought to be rid of them. For him, the important thing was to attain the relationship to God which seemed to him to be the right one. His failure to find his way out did not mean that the fault was his. It only revealed that the Catholic system of salvation and comfort was not adequate for the goal he had set for himself. It was adapted to the "moderate" moral needs of the average person, and

---

17. Before 1517 Luther does not use the word *attritio* at all. He always uses *contritio* for repentance. Whenever he uses *attritio* after 1517, he does so only to oppose this concept.

suited to the type of soul that could be satisfied with the divine assurance offered in the sacrament. Whoever, like Luther, examined even the faintest impulses of the heart in the consciousness that before God there are no secrets, and whoever did this, not in order to be able to confess perfectly but actually to get rid of the sin and to achieve the purity that alone is acceptable to God, would inevitably face difficulties that the church had pushed aside.

Luther's difficulties with the "awakened" act and contrition were really only the inevitable result of his conception of morality. They made him face the questions that had first dawned upon Paul, the great pioneer, and to which Søren Kierkegaard and Nietzsche, too, in his way, tried to direct people's minds in the nineteenth century. The basic issue in Luther's struggle was the practicality of moral effort oriented to an absolute standard. Luther personally experienced what Paul had spoken of as the impossibility of keeping the law. The reason the law cannot be kept is not only that its fulfillment lies beyond human power, but that the law itself increases sin. This was Luther's most disquieting discovery. The very desire to overcome sin through compliance with the unconditional command revivifies the power of sin. Penitent recollection of past sin also revives the desire that led to it. The intention to resist a particular sin makes a person fearful and all the more apt to fall. The more deliberately one seeks concentration, the more easily do one's thoughts wander. The appetite combatted by fasting asserts itself the more furiously. Luther had the crushing experience of feeling that, despite all his concern for holiness, he was becoming ever more base and insecure.

But this experience led him still further into perplexity. When, in his anguish, he thought of God, he could only picture him as the Judge who would punish him for his sins, and certainly for good reason. The knowledge of this inevitable judgment produced in him the torments of hell. When the Holy decisively confronted him, as perhaps in the sacrament of the altar, or in an image of Christ, it only served to frighten him. To advance from the feeling of dread to the feeling of hope, or at such a moment to induce an act of love to God as the church advocated, was an inner impossibility for him. How could he, unclean as he was, dare to ap-

40

proach God? Yet this failure to seek God merely added another sin. His most severe temptations occurred at this point. He spontaneously felt something like hatred rising in him against the God whose law imposed an unreasonable demand and then punished the failure to fulfill it. The doctrine of eternal election helped to nourish this feeling. Was not God really cruel if he granted his salvation arbitrarily to a portion of mankind and jealously cut off all hopes of salvation from the rest, even though they honestly strove after it? Luther fought against these thoughts as soon as they stirred within him. They were manifest blasphemies. But they kept coming back even when he suppressed them. This was the height of agony for him. It must surely be the fate of the damned in hell to have blasphemous thoughts and not be able to free themselves from them. In moments like these, Luther fell into that pit from which the church tried to protect its members by the moderation of its doctrine: he despaired.

Luther was not a voluntarist in the sense of an Ignatius of Loyola who, driven close to suicide by a similar affliction, flung aside all scruples with a mighty surge of courage. The way out which other afflicted souls had tried—the striving after visions or miraculous signs which would guarantee their personal pardon—would not do. Luther wanted no visions, for he did not like evasions. In all his perplexity, his conscience alone remained the unwavering rule by which he judged his relationship to God, and he was unwilling to have its power weakened in any way. The only possible solution for him was the discovery of a new side of God, particularly with respect to his attitude toward sin. The new view of God came to him as a surprise, as a sudden enlightenment. It came to him through Paul,[18] who opened Luther's eyes to the fact that all of his striving was a mistake. Personal union with God and recognition by God can never be won as the prize of human

18. All the other influences that affected Luther at this time—Augustine, Bernard, Tauler, Gerson, Staupitz—were ultimately significant only insofar as they led him to Paul. It must be remembered that all of these men, despite the deeper insights gained from Paul, had made their peace with the ordinary Catholic doctrines of the sacraments, merit, and satisfaction, and the distinction between mortal and venial sins. That Luther rejected these ideas was not due to them but, insofar as outside influences were involved at all, solely to Paul. . . .

struggle and sacrifice. We can never produce anything perfect enough to force God's hand. However, what cannot be extorted from him, God freely gives. We do not first seek God, God seeks us. God wants us in spite of our sin. He himself builds a bridge for us by his forgiveness. His pardon is as complete as his demand. This is precisely the meaning of the gospel. Luther had broken through the whole idea of conquering God and bargaining with him; instead, he felt himself conquered by God.

It was not merely the authority of the external word of the Bible which delivered Luther out of his anguish. We can see clearly how he was inwardly prepared for this decisive change. All his life he had maintained the view, which appears even in his early writings, that to think oneself farthest from God is actually to be closest to him. For someone to know God as the angry Judge is not as bad as the failure to perceive him at all. If God smites our conscience, it means that God is concerned about us and wants to win us. Luther could have learned this only by personal experience. There must have been a moment in which the presentiment flashed through the midst of his inner anguish that God, through this very torment, was seeking and drawing him to himself.[19] This thought led to his deliverance. In it he understood God. Now he saw through his pain the goodness of God. Here the purity of Luther's striving also becomes evident. He would never have been able to arrive at this interpretation of his experience if communion with God and divine sanctification had meant no more to him than his personal weal or woe. But in this new sense he dared to believe in the miracle of an unconditional pardon.

It is characteristic of Luther that this redeeming assurance did not lead him to regard his earlier dread of sin as an evil specter. What he had discovered about God's holiness and his unconditional demand remained unchanged for him. But now he saw a

---

19. Here again the difference between Luther and Gerson becomes palpable. In *De consolatione theologiae* Gerson comforts the troubled person with the thought that precisely as troubled and almost despairing he is in the proper attitude of humility toward God and thus is even pleasing to God; that is, he refers him to his humility as to a kind of merit. Luther, on the other hand, keeps to what is wrought in him by God.

way to achieve what he had previously tried in vain to do. He did not have to exert himself in order to "awaken" actual love for God. God himself had awakened that love by himself coming to the unworthy one. His goodness had conquered the heart of the one who was estranged. The only thing left to do was to yield to the effect of this wonderful love. The free, joyful love owed to God would then arise spontaneously. Moreover, it would be even stronger and purer, because it was connected with a deep inner shame. Paul's beautiful word regarding the "love of God which is shed abroad in our hearts," which had become the basis for the Scholastic idea of an incomprehensible and almost magical action of God, became for Luther a living experience. That warm feeling toward God which arose in him when he contemplated the mercy of God was actually a power given to him by God. Now he was ready to agree with Duns Scotus, the Nominalists, and Augustine when they identified this love of God with the Holy Spirit. He experienced this identity in the rapture that the love of God brought to his soul, and in the inner rejoicing in the good with which it filled him. Now the Holy Spirit was no longer something divorced from his experience, believed in merely for the sake of dogma, but something sensible and real in his own heart.

Thus his viewpoint became more firmly fixed. Looking back now from his new vantage point upon the course of his development, he came to a strange conclusion. The path he had taken had been a wrong path and yet not a wrong path. It was the path one had to take in order to understand clearly one's relationship to God. For Luther, forgiveness and the assurance of forgiveness now occupied the central place in Christianity. Scholasticism had regarded forgiveness only as something that prepares for or accompanies the infusion of power; for Luther, forgiveness was the key to everything else, the central concern. To conceive of God as the One who can and wants to forgive was to understand the most wonderful and profound truth about him. Its recognition, which secured one's relationship to God, was more important than everything else.

In order to attain to this recognition it was necessary, as Luther saw, for a person to follow a detour. The full meaning of for-

Anfechtung

giveness could be appreciated only by one who had come completely to the end of his powers. Luther attained clarity on this point as he developed Pauline conceptions regarding the meaning of the law, which he did as early as 1513 in his Lectures on the Psalms. He laid hold of the relationship between religion and morality at its deepest level. God has given us the law, the moral consciousness. It would seem, then, to be natural and even required that we should seek the acceptance of God through moral deeds. But the more earnestly we attempt this, the more certainly will we fall into despair; and this despair is just what God wants, as is proved by the fact that he forgives. Forgiveness has meaning only if a person is and remains a sinner before God. But we are supposed to try it alone first so that, despairing of ourselves, we will perceive that God alone is righteous and holy. Only in this way can the relationship between God and human beings be rightly ordered. This gift of moral apperception, the knowledge of good and evil, is always accompanied by the temptation to strive to "be like God," the vain belief that by ourselves we can be somebody and do something. Such arrogance must be rooted out completely. We must see clearly that at our best we are still nothing in God's sight. The pride that wants to rescue a bit of self and in some way to claim some goodness before God is the greatest barrier to reconciliation with God. This is no hyperbole but the plainest fact; it is waking up from a dream and learning to see through God's eyes when, precisely, by virtue of the moral knowledge we share with God, we perceive the absolute chasm between ourselves and God.

This insight exerted a transforming influence in two directions. On the one hand, Luther used it to discard the Catholic conception of merit and everything connected with it. He would not even tolerate it in the form in which Augustine and Thomas had retained it, namely, as a point of view that was permissible from within the human consciousness of freedom, though from God's vantage point good deeds were solely the result of grace. For Luther, there is only one approach—the one that corresponds to the judgment of God. According to that approach, human action

44

always falls short of God's requirement. What Lutheranism later expressed in its emphasis upon the *particulae exclusivae*, Luther already laid down here. For all it means is that in religion only the highest standard, God's own, may be employed. On the other hand, a new insight into the idea of judgment resulted. A person's confession of total sinfulness was not only a self-judgment. If it was made in the living presence of God, it was also a judgment leveled by God. Thereby "judgment" is transposed from the future into the present, into the realm of personal experience—as in the Johannine writings, whose words Luther actually uses. The awesome experience of the presence of God, which we dare not avoid but whose impact we must bear, becomes a necessary stage in our inner development. Indeed, this happens as often as God approaches us, for this judgment of God is repeated over and over again. More properly, it hangs over us continually. Luther is not trying to abolish the reality of the Last Judgment. It always stands behind the events of the present and serves as a reminder not to resort to the folly of self-deception.

Against the background of this direct experience of judgment, the full meaning of forgiveness stands out in bold relief. Now it is seen as the establishment of a divine-human relationship on an entirely new basis. It really is the establishment of a relationship and not merely the repair or improvement of an existing one. Yet Luther encountered a difficulty at this point which neither Scholasticism nor the mystics had noted sufficiently.[20] If God's judgment actually issued in a person's just condemnation, as Luther always emphasized, then forgiveness in spite of it was an incomprehensible miracle and should be seen as such, that is, as an

---

20. The importance of the mystics for Luther's inner development has just been emphasized once again, and indeed exaggerated, by Alfons V. Mueller, *Luther und Tauler auf ihren theologischen Zusammenhang neu untersucht* (1918); see Otto Scheel, "Taulers Mystik und Luthers reformatorische Entdeckung," *Festschrift für Kaftan* (1920), pp. 298ff. Even when Luther uses the very language of the mystics it has a unique ring. Like the mystics, he says that in the presence of God one should feel oneself to be absolutely unworthy, to be nothing. For the mystic, however, this is an artificial intensification of feeling, while Luther is convinced that it is simply the recognition of a fact. For that reason, guilt is a greater hindrance to reconciliation with God for Luther than it ever was for the mystics.

incomprehensible and free act of God. But how then could a person believe such forgiveness, especially after just frankly confessing oneself to be worthy of destruction?

Here something becomes apparent that is discernible in Luther's whole argument, namely, that he proceeds from his own personal experience in order to show that it corresponds to the realities involved. He expects that a person will first receive the message of God's grace only with suspicion. Therefore, he immediately places great emphasis on the indubitable fact of God's willingness to forgive. He overcomes the timidity that resists forgiveness as though it were something dangerous by pointing to the much greater danger involved in the refusal to accept forgiveness. The gospel announcing forgiveness is as truly a word of God as is the sentence of judgment, and must be taken just as seriously. In fact, to distrust the gospel is even worse than to rob God of his honor by opposing his judgment, for it means making God a liar and outraging him to the utmost by representing him as incapable of such goodness. Because of such offenses and barriers as must be overcome in the return to God, faith now acquires a special sense and increased importance. For Luther it means taking God seriously, acknowledging his veracity, both in his judgment of condemnation and in the gospel.[21] But such acknowledgment is inconceivable without an act of the will that includes the conquest of self. In the case of judgment it means to overcome pride; in the other, stupidity. Luther does emphasize intellectual acceptance, however, in order to affirm that assent to God, recognition of God alone as righteous and good, is the ultimately decisive factor. Faith, as this sort of assent, is the real proof of religion, for it "gives God the glory"—the highest possible glory and the only one he really demands. The love of God follows only upon such faith. In fact, such faith necessarily turns into love, for faith

---

21. Luther accordingly can use the words "humility" and "faith" interchangeably here, and can even combine the two in the expression *humilitas fidei*. The fact that Luther frequently says "humility" when he could just as well say "faith" caused Hartmann Grisar in childish jest to entitle one of his chapters "The Righteousness of Christ Appropriated by—Humility!" (Grisar, *Luther*, vol. 1, p. 172).

cannot be complete without the highest kind of "affect,"[22] without a powerful emotional attachment to God, which inevitably advances from obedience to God's gracious will to grateful devotion to the God of grace.

Corresponding to all this was a change in the concept of sin. If faith in the sense indicated is our basic duty, then unbelief, in whatever form, is the worst of all sins, whether it takes the form of despair and hatred of God, of murmuring against God and his law, or above all of pride. Already at this point Luther takes pride more seriously than the sins designated as mortal by the church. More precisely, pride emerges from the list of seven deadly sins with a new meaning that goes even beyond Augustine. As the refusal unconditionally to accept God's offer of forgiveness, it is the fundamental sin against God.

All this involved a general advance over Scholasticism. The processes through which Luther attained his certitude about God were all of a conscious, intellectual, personal sort. Faith in God, such as Luther now held to be a duty, could never arise from a sacrament that exerts its influence somewhere beneath the level of the conscious. Just as his guilt stood clearly before him, so release from it could only take place through something distinct and public, that is, through a "word." But not through the mere word of a priest. It had to be a word of God, and one that attested itself as such by its own character. This leap to personal assurance at the same time broke through sacramental magic and advanced to the intellectual apprehension of God.

These were the fundamental principles that gave rise to Luther's new overall concept of religion. There can be no doubt that in him the unmitigated impulses of primitive Christianity came alive again with triumphant power. Contrasted with the prevailing doctrine, these impulses signified a revolution that touched the very heart of the religious consciousness, and Luther possessed the energy to work out their full implications. The fact that in this

22. I put "affect" in quotation marks as a reminder that Luther always presupposed the peculiar Nominalistic doctrine of the soul. He, too, only distinguishes between *intellectus* and *affectus*; the will is accordingly included in the latter.

process he strongly emphasized his opposition to the Catholic interpretation of religion did not, of course, preclude his conscious and subconscious retention of whatever he found valuable in the medieval development. Nor did his going back to primitive Christianity prevent him from purging it of many of the remaining vestiges of earlier stages of religious development.

4. Luther's Religion: A Religion of Conscience

Luther's religion is a "religion of conscience"[23] in the most pronounced sense of the word, with all the urgency and the personal character belonging to it. It issues from a particular kind of conscientious experience—namely, his unique experience of the conflict between a keen sense of responsibility and the unconditional, absolute validity of the divine will—and rests on the conviction that in the sense of obligation (*sollen*), which impresses its demands so irresistibly upon the human will, divinity reveals itself most clearly; and the more profoundly a person is touched by the obligation and the more sharply it contrasts with one's "natural" desires, the more lucid and unambiguous is the revelation. It is a basic principle with Luther that it is not what a person freely devises or "chooses" that bears the stamp of the divine but rather what is imposed by a higher order, something that has to be done. For it is precisely this imposed obligation—in tension with the natural desire for life, and therefore regarded as "foolishness" by one who seeks only happiness—that causes one to sense that the deeper, true meaning of life is concealed in it.[24] The law, says Luther, transcends reason;[25] that is, obligation goes beyond the

---

23. Luther himself used this expression: "The way to heaven is the line of an indivisible point, namely of the conscience" (*WA* 40[1], p. 21, l. 12).

24. I deliberately avoid using the now popular word "irrational" (even though it contains a valid idea) because it is too ambiguous. Max Weber (*The Protestant Ethic and the Spirit of Capitalism* [New York: Scribner, 1930], pp. 193–94, n. 9) has rightly reminded us that both "irrational" and

mere calculation of utility and consequences. As over against his own "rational" striving, Luther perceives the emergence in himself of another, unconditional will, which he is bound to distinguish from his own and yet cannot avoid recognizing as right. Thus the concept of God, and specifically of a personal God, is for Luther directly connected with the sense of obligation.[26] It is precisely this kind of pressure that forms the basis of Luther's certitude that he is dealing not with a fiction but with the living God.

Luther's view signifies a delimitation in two directions. First of all, it means that Luther rejected the pantheistic tendency of mysticism. For him, religion could never be a matter of discovering himself to be God. As religion of conscience, his religion was a community of will, a relationship of one will to another. But at the same time Luther also felt himself lifted beyond the philosophical difficulties with which Scholasticism wrestled. He never regarded the epistemological questions raised by Scotus and the Nominalists, questions so significant in their own way, as worthy of discussion. He did not need that kind of foundation. To Luther, God himself proved his existence directly in the conscience. But from the outset he also suspected that all philosophical discussion of theological matters would lead to a God entirely different from the God of Christianity. The God who corresponds to "reason" could only be the God of works-righteousness. For "reason" must maintain the principle that God

---

"rational" are relative concepts that depend on the presupposed norm. Accordingly, "irrational" can have many shades of meaning. From the standpoint of eudaemonism strict morality is "the irrational"; ethics, on the other hand, regards the natural instinct as "irrational." For me, however, there is a more important consideration. What is decisive is not that religion is "irrational," or, to use an older and probably better expression, "paradoxical." If religion were nothing more than this, it would be an absurdity. The important consideration is that religion provides meaning, that it at least hopes for a final unraveling of those things which at first seem unintelligible. . . .

25. *WA* 40[1], p. 306, l. 3: "The giving of the law is to bring enlightenment above human reason (*supra rationem hominis*) and to declare what is to be done."

26. Undoubtedly Luther would have had only contempt for the sentimentality of a "religion without God." Honest atheism, because it is genuine, is always more honorable than a substitute religion that has no real object for its "feelings of awe."

is pleased with one who strives for a "blameless" way of life. A God who is concerned for the sinner is incomprehensible from this point of view.

Luther therefore emphasized all the more that religion—precisely when it is understood as religion of conscience—addresses itself to personal freedom, to personal decision. Nowhere did it seem to him so important to emphasize freedom as in religion. Even the relationship to God seemed to him genuine and true only when based upon personal conviction. Here he differed decisively from the view of the Catholic church, which had confidence that the practice of the masses, guided by their instinct, was unconditionally right, and accordingly regarded as pious the willingness to relinquish to others responsibility for one's own actions. Luther, on the other hand, regards the willingness to bear personal responsibility as a test of the sincerity of one's religion. The situation may arise, therefore, where the individual's God-consciousness is to be affirmed even over against the entire group.

The grounding of religion in conscience also implied that in the order of ideas the concept of God should become the governing one. If religion is primarily obligation, then it is necessary first of all to explain the will that stands behind this obligation. Luther's thinking is strictly "theocentric."[27] While for the philosopher, God is the ultimate concept that is reached only after the world and humanity, for Luther, God is the point of departure first enabling him to apprehend both.

27. There has been a good deal of controversy recently about "theocentrism" and "anthropocentrism," without a corresponding degree of clarity having been attained. The profound wisdom that the whole content of human consciousness is in the first instance a human possession and thus all thought, including religious thought, is anthropocentric really should not have been pressed. Does it not matter in what sequence, in what order, notions are presented? A theocentric approach is characterized by two things. In the first place, the concept of God is not conditioned by our understanding of human nature (or claims); rather, our concept of what it means to be human is conditioned by the concept of God, that is, what God is is not determined by "postulates" but is used to determine human "possibility" (or impossibility). In the second place, religion is not based on human desires or needs but on the "ought," the duty imposed on us by God. May I remind today's dogmatic theologians that Christoph Schrempf, in his first published work, *Die christliche Weltanschauung und Kants sittlicher Glaube* (Göttingen, 1891), which is still worth reading, was the first to clarify this question and to struggle against the prevailing viewpoint for a theocentric approach.

Luther's conception of God faithfully reflected what he had experienced. It was natural, however, that what he had found to be the ultimate concept should come first in his objective reconstruction. He had finally come to understand God as the One who draws to himself, that is, as love, and he was convinced that he had thereby caught a glimpse into the very heart of God.[28] But another

28. This is the place to define more closely the significance for Luther of Christ as the revealer of God. Luther often enough enunciated the principle that one must not begin by "speculating" about the "majesty" of God, but that God must be sought where he has made himself known: in Christ, or, more precisely, in the human Christ. See, for instance, *WA* 40¹, p. 75, ll. 9ff.: "You have often heard that this rule should be urged in reference to the Holy Scriptures, that we ought to abstain from the speculation of the majesty . . ."; ibid., p. 76, l. 9: "You are not required to ascend to God; rather begin where he began: in the mother's womb 'he became human and came into being'; and restrain the speculative mind . . ."; ibid., p. 602, l. 5: "God only wants to be known through Christ . . . he is the mirror (*speculum*), the means, the way whereby we know God . . . this is the divine report that does not deceive but defines God in a sure form; outside of it there is no God." *WA* 50, p. 267, ll. 5ff.: "For thus it was decreed, says St. Paul, that in Jesus Christ the whole, entire Godhead was to dwell, bodily and personally. Hence, whoever does not find or apprehend God in Christ shall nevermore and nowhere find or apprehend God outside Christ, though he should travel above heaven, below hell, outside the world." This is the basis of the opinion, represented especially within the Ritschlian school, that Luther based his entire faith in God on the authority of Christ.

But we must take a closer look at the sense in which Luther forbids "speculation" about the majesty of God, and at what the "majesty" of God means to him in this connection. In every case where Luther speaks in this manner, the question is how to enter into relationship with God or how to conquer *Anfechtung*. *WA* 40¹, p. 77, ll. 3ff.: "In this matter, how to act with God and toward God and against sin and death, let go the speculation of the majesty . . ."; ibid., p. 78, ll. 8ff.: "But in the matter of righteousness, against sin, death, and devil . . . there one must simply abstain from thoughts and speculations of the majesty . . ."; ibid., p. 79, l. 10: "When you want to act, think of your salvation. . . ." In that case one must not make the God of majesty his starting point. For the God of majesty is not some "God in his essence" [*Gott "an sich"*] or some God conjured up by speculation (as we use the term) but the God of *moral* majesty, the God who states his demands and judges us accordingly. This God could crush us. *WA* 40¹, p. 77, l. 5: "Let God go, because he is unbearable (*intolerabilis*) here. . . ." As the God of majesty, God is our enemy. Drews, *Disputationen*, p. 268: "In his nature and majesty, God is our adversary; he presses the demands of the law and threatens the transgressors with death . . ."; ibid., p. 294: "Whoever forsakes the Son, to follow his own thoughts and speculations, is drowned by the majesty of God, and despairs." If, therefore, one desires to "find" God, that is, if one wants to be united with him, one must confine oneself to the God who has revealed himself in Christ as the love that seeks us, as pardoning mercy. To show God in this way is Christ's "proper" work. . . . Drews, *Disputationen*, p. 300: "Christ's proper work is to announce grace and the remission of sins." This God is not merely the only one we can "bear," he is also the true, the "real" God.

Luther evidently does not want to push the God of majesty (as he under-

aspect of God's nature, which had likewise become important in his experience, immediately collided with this love. Luther's conscience had led him to recover the Pauline doctrine of the wrath of God which had been suppressed in the West, mainly by Augus-

stands him) completely aside. What is still more important, however, is that he likewise does not regard the proclamation of grace as the sole work of Christ. By speaking of Christ's "proper" office, Luther already hints that he also knows of another office of Christ. This other office is the interpretation of the law. WA 40¹, p. 259, ll. 11ff.: "But as for the precepts contained in it—these are the appendices of the gospel . . . when Christ is the lawgiver regarding sin, he increases people's burden . . ."; ibid., p. 568, l. 9: "That he indeed gives precepts—put that down somewhere else . . ."; Drews, Disputationen, p. 378: "He interprets the law perfectly and spiritually . . ."; ibid., p. 388: ". . . where Christ interprets the law spiritually." Normally Luther ascribes this office to Moses, in order then to set Moses the giver of law over against Christ the herald of grace. But this is only possible for him when he reads the "spiritual sense" of the law—that is, the sense which he himself also had discovered only in the Sermon on the Mount—back into Moses. Whenever he admits that it was Christ who "interpreted" the law, Luther's judgment is not only historically more correct, but also more in keeping with his own inner development.

For Luther, the significance of Christ is thus twofold. In the first place, Christ is the one who shapes the human conscience by giving a definite content and a sure goal to the natural sense of duty. Particularly, it must not be forgotten that Luther's conception of law and conscience always includes first of all a consciousness of duty to God. See, for instance, Drews, Disputationen, p. 378: "Yet neither was Moses the author of the Decalogue; but since the world was made, the Decalogue has been inscribed in the minds of all human beings . . . for there never was a nation so cruel, barbarous, and inhuman as not to sense that God ought to be worshiped and loved, and his name be praised, even if it erred with respect to the mode and the motives of the worship of God; the same is true of the honor and obedience to be shown to parents; likewise were vices detested."

In the second place, Christ is the one who reveals God's forgiveness, as opposed to the law. . . . On the one hand, Luther stresses that Christ does not merely "proclaim," but that he "does" a work, and specifically a work by which he proves himself to be God. See WA 40¹, p. 81, ll. 2ff.: "Christ does not bring peace as the apostles did, by preaching it, but by giving it; the Father gives and makes the remission of sins, and peace; Christ also gives these same things . . . ; but to give grace and the remission of sins and life and justification and freedom from death and from one's sins—these are not the works of a creature but of the one, sole majesty; angels cannot justify me, nor liberate me from death or remit my sins; all these things pertain to the glory of the supreme majesty of the Creator; and yet it was for Christ to give and create them; therefore he must be very God." Luther thus bases faith in the deity of Christ not on his miracles but on something that can be experienced by anyone today, namely, the creative influence exercised by Christ upon the human heart through his word of grace. But on the other hand Luther equally stresses, in apparent contradiction to the point just made, that Christ revealed and did not his own will but the will of the Father. He leads us not to himself but to the Father. WA 40¹, p. 98, ll. 10ff.: "How often he brings blessings to us, that through his words and deeds we might come to understand not so much Christ himself but the Father. He comes in order to apprehend us—with our eyes fixed upon him we are drawn and led by the right road to

tine.[29] It corresponded to his sober sense of God's holiness. God must be angry with—that is, he must condemn—not only the sinner but also the relatively righteous person, for with God there is no intermediate ground between Yes and No: only that which is perfect can stand before him; he can only reject and annihilate the imperfect.

The reintroduction of this doctrine of the wrath of God gave a new turn not only to Luther's view of God but also to his view of the world. As over against the mystics, who saw in the world only a shadow of reality, Luther vigorously affirmed the real, autonomous existence of the world when he represented it as the object

---

the Father, because this is not to be obtained by speculation, nor is it to be hoped that anything of a saving nature can be known of God the Father where Christ is not apprehended. Christ, then, shows me this grace not of his own will but of the Father's." What ultimately matters, therefore, is how the Father is disposed.

Now we are in a position to see what service Christ renders the believer. It does not consist in a simple overriding of all doubts by the authority of Christ, and certainly not in the establishment of faith in God on the sole basis of this authority. For there is, after all, a certain ambiguity in Christ himself. He confronts us with a similar question as does God. Because he is also a proclaimer of law, one can . . . regard him as a judge and fear him accordingly. See *WA* 40[1], p. 298, l. 9: "I grew pale when I heard the name of Christ." Very valuable is Luther's admission that this conception remained with him into his old age. Drews, *Disputationen,* p. 478: "Nor am I able today to look upon my Lord Jesus with the kind of glad countenance he desires, because I was imbued with that pestilent doctrine that portrayed God as angry at us, and Christ as a judge." Elsewhere Luther could express the same idea by saying that since Christ is also God, he, too, is "majesty." *WA* 40[1], p. 92, ll. 9ff.: "It is indeed true that Christ is the future judge, I cannot deny it . . . then I am afraid of Christ." See ibid., p. 93, l. 5: "There he becomes the true Christ; so I relinquish the speculation of the majesty and cleave to the humanity, and then I am not afraid of his being God." But how legitimate, then, is it for the believer to regard the preaching of grace as the "proper" work of Christ and the proclamation of the law as a mere appendage? Luther, too, was aware that this question required an answer; it could flow only from an ultimate, immediate certainty.

In Luther's view there is actually an interaction; each element supports the other. Christ's preaching of grace presents to us an idea that is contrary to all "reason" and to his own preaching of the law; the idea, namely, that God wants to forgive. The word has a comforting effect, but for this very reason also arouses distrust. Its power to carry full conviction is derived only from the feeling that the God who can forgive and who wants to bestow new life is greater, is "God" in a truer sense, than one who merely judges and casts down. This feeling springs up out of the innermost depths of personal being—Luther would say that it is wrought by the Holy Spirit. . . .

29. The very fact that Luther is here *reviving* an idea dooms every attempt to present his doctrine in such a way as to make the wrath of God not a reality in God but only a reflection in the human consciousness. Luther of course rejected the anthropomorphic implications of the concept. . . .

of God's wrath. Even more important, Luther thus rejected the aesthetic element that had insinuated itself into the Christian concept of God from Neoplatonism. He also broke with the view that regarded the richness of God as an essential, if not the outstanding, attribute of God, and which admired this richness in the variety of levels of being coexisting in the world. For him, as for primitive Christianity, the only valid basis for a world-view was the unconditional ethical standard.

While Luther affirmed the coexistence in God of wrath and love, it confronted him with a very serious question. He had no intention of carrying his notion of God's wrath to the point where God could only condemn and destroy the developing life in the world, which is, after all, God's own creation. The concept of divine love opposed such a view. But Luther was no more inclined to suspend or weaken the concept of wrath by means of the concept of love. Both wrath and love had to be upheld in all their fullness. Yet he felt constrained to seek the unity behind the antithesis. A word of Scripture gave him the answer. It was the passage in which Isaiah (28:21) speaks of wrath as an "alien" or "strange" work of God. From this, Luther concluded that wrath and love in God are not on the same level. Love is his "proper" work, wrath is not. Wrath is the mask behind which God hides himself. It belongs to God's nature that he reveals himself even in his antithesis. He does this, however, not out of caprice but according to a definite plan. God uses wrath to accomplish his goal, to dispose of the hindrances that stand in the way of the complete achievement of his highest purpose. For in comparison with the ultimate, the totally perfect, even the partially perfect is a barrier, a stop along the way.

It is very important, however, to distinguish between the types of wrath. There is a severe and destructive wrath that is designed only to punish. It reveals itself in the Last Judgment, but also in the present wherever God rejects what is totally useless. There is also, however, a "wrath of mercy" that purges and liberates. This is experienced by the person whom God afflicts in the judgment of the conscience. Here a person is shattered by God, but only in order to be transformed and recreated. God must shatter again and again those to be drawn up to himself, who are to share his own nature with him. In this way, in and through wrath, a love is revealed which desires the ultimate for people and which works tirelessly to this end. This is a more profound and manlike conception than the one that seems so similar—"everything that exists is worthy of being destroyed." Behind the annihilation, Luther sees a coming-to-be, behind the destruction a creation, the emergence of something eternal in the perishing of the finite. At the same time, one can see how Luther's concept of love is deepened by its connection with wrath. Strength of will and wholesome severity give to love a pedagogical dimension. Love now is understood as a power that does not hesitate to inflict hurt in order to liberate its object from itself and to raise it above itself. One need only compare Luther's with Tolstoy's weak conception in order to see the greatness of Luther's interpretation.

But Luther delved even more deeply into the concept of God. He was certain that in his understanding of God's love he not only had found the unifying factor of the concept of God, but also had exhibited the innermost, the deepest reality in God. He thereby sublated the Catholic concept of God, which Duns Scotus had only carried to its logical conclusion. Luther's certainty meant that there is no transcendent "ground" in God which is more sublime than his love, on which—or on the decision of which—his love would depend. Nor is God, as Duns Scotus and in somewhat different fashion the German mystics pictured him, an indeterminate being who only through arbitrary self-limitation (or self-unfolding) maintains form, stature, and purpose. He is determinate from the beginning—as love. Love is his "nature," it is the very essence of God himself. God can never will anything except with love in view.

A limitation of God seemed to be implied here. But Luther was able to show that on this basis he had attained to a much more profound concept of the absoluteness of God than that of the Catholic church. For, he said (and here he struck at the root of the weakness in the Catholic concept of God), the greatness of God does not consist in the fact that he is enthroned on high in blessed solitude, independent of both the world and humanity.

Rather, he is great because he is able to produce autonomous life outside himself and to guide it upward to himself. Everyone recognizes that the true master is not the one who keeps his ability to himself and knows only how to shame the bungler but the one who knows how to pass his ability along to others. Or put even more simply, God proves himself to be God most conclusively when he dispenses blessings, for thus he shows himself to be the One who can always give, who alone can really give, and who is generous enough always to be first with his gifts. That God does this is his prerogative and his "glory." Luther tries to exhaust all of the implications of this view. If God in his innermost being is love, then this also means that he is unceasingly active. The old formula of God as the *actus purus* receives a new and fuller meaning with Luther. God is not the One who contemplates himself and enjoys himself; he is not primarily thought but will and action. He "never rests." As he has set his goal from eternity, so he works without ceasing toward it, creating and elevating the creation. For that reason he is called the Living One. But again, his life is nothing else than love; God acts and lives by imparting himself. His perfection is to reproduce it in others as in his images. As he himself is holy, so he makes people holy; as he is righteous, he makes them righteous; as he is wise, he makes them wise. He is "the spring forever overflowing with goodness." Therefore, in virtue of his nature—not "contingently," as the Scholastics said—he wants a world, he wants people, in order to pour his love into them.

Luther incorporated this systematic aiming of the will toward a goal directly into the concept of God. But he did not forget the other aspect, that God also possesses absolute power to carry out his will. Luther understood God so deeply that he actually "endured" him. He did not engender his own agonies of conscience; God produced them in him. Nor did he then raise himself up again; God raised him up. Even in his daily activities he experienced the same thing. In the very moments when he ventured to be most daring, he felt most strongly that he was only acting under a necessity that was laid upon him. "We do not act, we are being acted upon." Faith in the divine monergism was not a piece of doctrine which Luther had simply taken over from Paul; it grew out of his personal experience.[30] But what he had observed in himself now became a universal insight that changed his whole view of the world. The world now no longer appeared to him as the static order that it had been for the Greeks and the Scholastics. He saw it as in the process of never-ceasing movement, and its order as being created anew at every moment. Thus he was able for the first time really to visualize the vitality of God, for it was God who, as "the restless driver," unceasingly promoted both action and interaction. The whole world was an uninterrupted testimony to his inexhaustible creative power. Therefore Luther, unlike the Scholastics, did not see God's omnipotence only in extraordinary events by means of which God broke through his established order. The ordinary course of the world was for him the greatest miracle. Omnipotence to him was not the infinite number of possibilities God had at his free disposal, but rather the infinite power shaping the existing world. It was manifest to him everywhere and always. The whole creation is God's mummery: the creatures are masks behind which God conceals himself, or tools with which he works.

Yet Luther's own relationship to this whole activity was not that of a spectator who merely observes from without. He felt himself included in it and affected by it, indeed directly produced by it; that is, by God: "I believe that God has created *me*." Without any hesitation, therefore, he inferred the bondage of the human will from God's omnipotence. Whereas Scotus wanted to affirm a "both—and," Luther saw only an "either—or": either the divine or the human will was free; either God was really omnipotent and in comparison human beings counted for nothing, or else they had a measure of independence and then God was not really omnipotent. For every attempt to save a space where the human will might freely exert itself even over against God—Luther insisted

30. Luther advocated the doctrine of divine monergism [*Alleinwirksamkeit*] explicitly only since the Lectures on Romans. But the decisive impulses toward it are already noticeable in the Lectures on the Psalms. . . .

sharply on this point—would not simply limit the divine omnipotence but abolish it and reduce God to the level of a mere world spectator.

Now this conclusion also forced Luther to consider the questions inherent in such a concept of God: natural evil, wickedness, and finally predestination. It was relatively easy for him to deal with the problem of natural evil. Basically it had been settled for him by his view of the love of God. Once he recognized that one cannot make moral progress without being continually shattered—that is, apart from pain and agony—there was no need for theodicy. Such a need would arise only in an age that regarded happiness as the supreme good and pain as the least tolerable aspect of the world. But Luther did go on to ponder the further question, whether human progress could not have taken place without suffering, and he found an ingeniously simple answer; the only one, in fact, which can be given. He maintained that apart from the existence of evil, human beings would not even be able to recognize God as God. God must give us pain. For only the loss of benefactions makes us conscious of them and teaches us to appreciate the might as well as the goodness of the Creator.

The second problem Luther had to take much more seriously, namely, whether God, "who works all in all," is not also responsible for wickedness. He posed this question in its most acute form. The convenient Neoplatonic explanation of evil as a mere deficiency of being, in which even Scholasticism finally sought refuge, was never adopted by him. Wickedness as an act of the will was a reality, a human self-assertion against God. But how was such an assertion even conceivable in a world created by God and ruled by his omnipotence? Luther took an important step toward the solution that seems unavoidable from his point of view. He was familiar with the idea that under certain circumstances God himself allowed people to fall into grievous sin in order to save them, that is, in order to open their eyes and so to achieve their conversion. Luther even ventured to make a statement that was to rouse Calvin's anger when Servetus mockingly repeated it—that an omnipresent God is present even in hell, yes, even in Satan.[31] It would have been easy to draw the same conclusion with respect to wickedness as in regard to natural evil: God must produce wickedness in order to arouse awareness of the good, and so to arouse the conscience of mankind. Luther could have applied his favorite formula, that God engages in a "strange" work in order to further his "proper" work. But he could not bring himself to this conclusion. He obviously feared that with such an admission all moral precepts would be deprived of their rigor. How could it then be maintained that God desires only the good, and unconditionally hates wickedness? Luther modestly chose to leave this riddle unsolved and to acknowledge that a divine mystery was involved.

Yet the same question confronted him once again at another point. If God is almighty, why does he not free everyone from the power of evil? Here, too, Luther posed the question as acutely as the case demanded. He was not only concerned, as most theologians were, with the reason God did not lead all to beatitude—that always was secondary for him—but also with the more serious problem, why God did not make everyone receptive to the good. Again, a solution was available: the doctrine of the restoration of all things at which Paul had hinted and which Origen had developed on a grand scale. Although Luther must have been acquainted with it, he made no use of it. The sacrifice would have been too great. He would have had to surrender, or at least weaken, the idea of judgment which was so important to him, as well as the rigor of the feeling of personal responsibility. This he could not do. He adhered to the God who creates and judges, that is, who rejects whatever is useless.

Thus he had no alternative but to accept predestination. Yet even this solution did not work very well. It conflicted with another significant element of Luther's vision. How could the concept of a decree of God which damns a part of mankind from all eternity be reconciled with the conviction that the gospel offers

31. *WA* 18, p. 709, l. 18: ". . . When God, therefore, moves and works all things, he necessarily moves and works also in Satan and the ungodly." *WA*, TR 1, p. 101, l. 4: ". . . So then he is also in the devil? Yes, and essentially he is indeed even in hell. . . ."

salvation to everyone? Luther thought he could get help here by
following the precedent set in the treatise *On the Calling of the
Gentiles,* in distinguishing between a "revealed" and a "secret"
will in God.[32]

It has become customary to designate Luther's position with
reference to these questions as his "Ockhamism" and on this basis
to speak of an abiding residue of Scholastic thinking in Luther—
an interpretation which, it must be admitted, can be supported by
several obviously caustic or facetious utterances of his.[33] Certainly
Luther owed not a little to Ockham, or more accurately, to Scotus.
Without the significant preliminary work of Duns, Luther would
never have been able to construct nearly so vigorous a concept of
God as in fact he did. But it is an illusion to think that he finally
fell back again into Ockhamism after having surmounted it at the
very beginning in his concept of God: God is not indefinite will
but will defined as love. The meaning usually attached to "Ockhamism" was something very well known to Luther, the interpretation of the will of God as ultimately unfathomable caprice. But

32. Reinhold Seeberg is hardly right when he connects this distinction with
the *potentia absoluta* and *ordinata* of Scotus (Charles E. Hay, trans., *Text-
book of the History of Doctrines* [Philadelphia: Lutheran Publication Society, 1905], vol. 2, p. 151). The formation of Luther's concept was
originally occasioned by the treatise *On the Calling of the Gentiles. . . .*
But even a contemporaneous or subsequent influence of the Scotist distinction is improbable. Seeberg himself stresses the fact that Luther includes the Scotist doctrine among the worthless inventions of Scholasticism
(see *WA* 18, p. 719, l. 14). The intentions of the two parties differ widely.
Scotus wants to stress that God is not inwardly committed even to his work
of salvation. It is Luther's presupposition, on the other hand, that God
unalterably affirms his work of salvation and merely reserves to himself
the manner and measure of its actualization. . . .

33. Even Grisar (*Luther,* vol. 1, p. 104) noticed that that much-quoted
statement "For I belong to the faction of the Ockhamists, who contemn
qualifications and take all things in an absolute sense" (*WA* 6, p. 600, l.
11) is a witticism. Luther's own added comment, "that I may thus joke
in this folly," surely made it easy for him to see this. "Ockham, my dear
master" (*WA* 30², p. 300, l. 9) was also undoubtedly intended to be
ironical, and even the more serious statement, "My master, Ockham, was
an unsurpassed dialectician, but he lacked the grace of eloquence" (*WA,*
TR 2, p. 516, l. 5), must be read in its context; for Luther continues by
classifying Ockham with Duns and Thomas as "speculative" theologians
in contrast to the more highly esteemed "men of conscience," William of
Paris and Gerson. Elsewhere he calls him his teacher only to indicate that
he wants to have nothing to do with him: "My master, Ockham, who is
regarded by us as the most learned of them all, denies that it is found in
Holy Scripture that the Holy Spirit is necessary for the consummation of
a good work" (Drews, *Disputationen,* p. 341).

wherever Luther encountered this interpretation he firmly disavowed it. As soon as he saw that any theological opinion implied arbitrariness in God he would dismiss it as untenable.

For the affirmation of the reality of the divine will is not Luther's last word. It sounds very Ockhamistic, to be sure, when he asserts that God is subject to no law and that therefore whatever he does is right because he does it. Luther's purpose in making this statement, however, is entirely different from Ockham's; in fact, it is the very opposite. For in contradistinction to Ockham and Duns, Luther is thoroughly convinced that God's action is always truly "right," that is, it has meaning—a meaning that we, too, will some day comprehend. Luther is concerned to provide practical proof for this conviction. Just as Christian faith sees the paradox that the righteous suffer most—which was quite beyond the grasp of pre-Christian thought—resolved into a demonstration of God's great goodness even in this life, so the problem of predestination will surely be solved on the higher plane of eternity. The election of one portion of mankind and the reprobation of the other, which "rational" thought now regards as a crying injustice, will be shown to be the highest kind of justice. It should be noted that Luther is not speaking from the Pharisaic standpoint of one fully assured of his own election, for he requires that even the nonelect recognize the judgment of God upon them as just, and he earnestly applies this to himself. Nor is his reference to the solution in eternity mere idle talk. He knows, as Scotus and Ockham did not, of an action that is completely free, independent of every law, and yet—or rather, for this very reason—most perfectly just.

In Luther's conception of morality this combination of supreme freedom and the supreme appropriateness of an action plays a most important role. It is the proper goal of human striving. Luther conceives of God's action in predestination similarly, and he thinks that he can expect the believer to interpret the apparent caprice as a real, though still hidden, justice. For if it is one of the first truths we are supposed to learn in the encounter with God—a truth confirmed by every conscience—that God is the Just One while all human beings are unjust, then a "bias of faith" will necessarily follow from it, namely, that God deals justly even where we cannot immediately comprehend the meaning of the divine action. There is so little question of Ockhamism here that one must say that, on the contrary, Luther's rather unique conception of God has passed its most crucial test: God is still seen as the will that always effects what is right and perfect, both in wrath and in love. Luther feels strong enough to maintain this faith even when he cannot prove it.

He does not regard the fact that mysteries still remain in his concept of God as a weakness but as a definite part of its strength.[34] It is part of God's majesty that there is much we do not know about him. If his being were completely transparent to us, he would really no longer be God. The desire to lift the last veil from God always arises out of the disposition that seeks to "be like God." But "a servant is not to know his lord's secret." The distance between human beings and God must be guarded in spite of the closeness of the intercourse between them. The grandeur of God is also expressed in the fact that the meaning of his will is always partly beyond our grasp.

5. Luther's Religion: A Religion of Selfless Selfhood

What form does a personal religion that is built upon this basis take? What is to be a person's position in relation to this kind of God? How are we to experience the various aspects of this concept of God in our own life? Luther first drew the simple and basic conclusion that we owe God religious service; and he drew it from the fact that God is will—a will that embraces us in its omnipotence, but that proves its goodness by bestowing life and implanting a higher destiny. Luther meant this in a dual sense:

34. Today the idea of "the mystery element in religion" is abused just like the idea of "the irrational." Some even go so far as to say that religion is *the* mystery. However, a religion that is no more than a mystery is really no religion at all, but at best obeisance to the "unknown god" about whom one hardly needs to be concerned. . . .

first, that there is a duty to be religious, indeed, that our supreme duty is our obligation to recognize and conform to our Creator, and conversely, that the practice of religion must always be regarded as a duty.

This implied, first of all, a sharp distinction between religion and the natural desire for life and happiness. Luther observed very early how important a role the desire for happiness played in the prevailing piety. At every turn he saw that the basic motive for piety was no more than a hunger for life and happiness: in the zeal for good works which God was to reward, in the endeavor to attain a relatively high degree of beatitude, in the veneration of saints and their invocation in time of need, and in the rush to get into the various competing brotherhoods. His contemporaries found this inoffensive and even natural. The opposition to it which had arisen among the mystics exerted no deep influence even upon the theologians. Since the time of Augustine it had been thought natural that people should seek their own bliss, their own happiness, in religion. To be sure, it was also said that they have the duty of honoring God. Augustine himself had not only coined the phrase that we must not "use" God, that is, make him a means to an end; he had also demanded that we should love God "for his own sake." But Augustine never interpreted these expressions so as to exclude or even restrain the idea of personal happiness. He naively believed that self-love attains its own fulfillment precisely in this kind of love to God.[35] The medieval theologians saw even less conflict between their admonition to love God for his own sake and their constant practical premise that attainment of beatitude is always the goal of the Christian's striving. One's duty to God seemed to be discharged by the recognition that the highest happiness could be found only in God.

Luther regarded it as his initial task to open the eyes of Christians on this point. It is immediately obvious that for him everything depended on the purity of the ultimate motives. To allow the desire for happiness was for him the sign of religion's degradation and its reversion to paganism. In paganism the will to live

---

35. See my essay "Augustins innere Entwicklung" [Augustine's inner development], *GA* 3, p. 107.

had always provided the impetus for religion; but there the gods were simply the reflection of human desires. "Those of the heathen whose desires were for power and dominion made Jove their highest god; others who desired wealth, fortune, or pleasure and good days preferred Hercules, Mercury, Venus or others. . . . Everybody made what was in his heart into his god."[36] Luther notes shrewdly that the fear of a god accompanying the desire for happiness in all pagan religions produces the same result—one's

36. *WA* 30¹, p. 135, ll. 1ff. It is necessary to take this occasion to touch also on the interpretation given by Georg Wobbermin (*Festschrift für Kaftan* [1920], pp. 418ff.) to the preceding remarks of Luther concerning "what it means to have a God, or what God is." Wobbermin thinks that Luther secured the "objective import" of the religious experience, that is, the certainty that religion is not a mere illusion, by relating it "to the historically objective foundation of religion." I forbear to discuss the question whether such a relating would in fact secure the "objective import" of religion. My only concern is with what Luther actually said in the place in question. Luther comes to the point when he says: "If your faith and confidence are right, your God is also right; and again, where the confidence is false and wrong, the right God is not there either." The decisive point is accordingly what he means by "right" confidence. In any case, what is meant is not "complete" confidence, for the latter could also refer to a false god, *WA* 30¹, p. 134, l. 5: "To have a god means to have something in which the heart reposes complete confidence." The difference between "right" and "wrong" confidence must be found at a deeper level. Luther makes no mention whatever of the "historically objective foundation of religion." Instead, he provides an interpretation by means of two sentences that substantially say the same thing: "Now you easily understand what and how much this commandment requires, namely, our whole heart and all our confidence in God alone and in no one else; for 'to have God' surely implies that he cannot be grasped and seized with your fingers nor put in a bag or locked up in a trunk . . ." (ibid., l. 18); "Now there you have what it is to glorify and serve God aright, in a manner pleasing to him, which he also commands on pain of eternal wrath, namely, that the heart should know no other comfort or confidence than in him, not allowing itself to be separated from it, but giving it first place over all earthly things and risking all for its sake" (ibid., l. 30). "Right" confidence is accordingly characterized by two moments: first, the confidence must be directed to a God who is truly transcendent, beyond the visible world; second, the "confidence" must be free from earthly wishes, from eudaemonistic desires. This second mark is still further underscored by the passage adduced in the text.
Luther regards the knowledge of the transcendent God himself as immediately given with the *syntheresis,* the conscience. See *Römerbrief* 2, p. 19, ll. 3ff.: "In this they erred, therefore, that they did not leave this deity in its nudity and worship it, but changed it and used it according to their own wishes and desires. And everyone wanted to find divinity in whatever pleased him, and thus they changed the truth of God into a lie. They therefore knew that it belongs to divinity, or to him who is God, to be powerful, invisible, just, immortal, good; they therefore knew the invisible things of God, his eternal power and godhead. This major [premise] of the *syllogismus practicus,* this theological *syntheresis,* is inobscurable in all. But in the minor [premise] they erred."

service to a god and therefore also one's god are shaped by the fancies of one's own heart. The fact that paganism pursued temporal goods while the current religiosity aspires after an eternal good makes no difference to Luther, for the decisive thing is that in seeking happiness we ultimately always seek ourselves. Luther sees more clearly than the mystics that even the desire for beatitude is always a selfish one.[37] As soon as this motive in religion is stressed or even allowed, the whole divine-human relationship is actually inverted. God becomes the servant whom we summon for our own purposes. Yet God does not exist for our sake, but we for God's. For God is the Creator and Lord and it is his right to demand submission. If religion is to be what it claims to be— service to God, and the fulfillment of a duty to him—then it must be completely divorced from the desire for salvation or happiness. Whoever longs for God's kingdom only in order to be saved will surely never enter it. God will have nothing to do with "favor-seekers" interested in him only for their own selfish ends.

Luther clarified this conception by means of a comparison with the New Testament idea of reward. To be sure, God rewards faithful service.[38] But this reward must come "by itself." It is given only to those who do not seek it. Where the prospect of reward becomes the motive, obedience to God is adulterated. What kind of son is it that obeys his father only because he hankers after the inheritance? Luther does not go to the extreme of labeling the idea of happiness as in itself sin, but in his view it always creates mischief in religion. He holds that the genuinely

---

37. Heinrich Denifle sheds light on the modern Roman Catholic interpretation when he writes with the intention of refuting Luther (*Luther und Lutherthum*, 2d ed., vol. 1, p. 672): "Everything else apart, *fiducia*, as the concept itself implies, is much more egoistic . . . than love. *Fiducia* involves no total surrender to God but rather a manipulation of God. It can no more justify a person than can faith alone." Worth noting is the admission that even love, according to the Catholic view, always has an egoistic element in it. Even more striking is the assertion, which is regarded as self-evident, that *fiducia,* in the sense of manipulating God, is necessarily selfish. Obviously, Denifle cannot even imagine a trust that is totally devoid of regard for one's personal welfare and that is unreserved surrender to God.

38. *Römerbrief* 2, p. 217, ll. 27ff.: "But those who truly love God with filial love and the love that prevails among friends . . . freely offer themselves to the whole will of God, even to eternal death and hell, if God should so will it; only in order that his will may be fully done."

pious individual would be willing to renounce heaven and be damned in hell if this should be God's will. "Whom have I in heaven but Thee? And there is none on earth that I desire beside Thee." Never has this doctrine been preached more forcefully.

Luther also avoided a reintroduction of the eudaemonistic motive he had initially expelled, which might compensate the renunciation of happiness in this life with a greater gain in the life to come. He transformed the whole concept of beatitude. For him it was not an enjoyment in addition to one's relationship to God; it was the unity of the will with God. It was the joyous feeling that spontaneously accompanies union with God and activity in accord with his will. This is true both in this life and in the life to come. Anyone who is really in earnest about finding God and becoming united with him will not desire anything else. Luther thereby excluded all childish expectations about the afterlife as well as all anticipation of a sensually conceived salvation, such as the delightful ecstasies of the mystics, the "Dionysian" experiences, and especially the intrusion into religion of erotic elements. For this reason Luther soon discarded even the expression "to enjoy God" which he initially borrowed from Augustine.

Luther did not want to base religion on the desire for benefits[39] or on any will originating in us, but rather on the impress that is given by God, which lays hold of us and shatters us in our feeling of selfhood. If God is in every instance the Alpha and Omega, then genuine religion can arise only when he makes himself perceptible to us, afflicts us with his severity, and actually crushes us. It is the sensation of the majesty of God, of "the Holy,"[40] to use the expression currently in vogue, which then begins to do its work

---

39. Feuerbach's analysis of religion accordingly applies only to what Luther himself calls "heathen" religion. This rejection of the natural desire to live and the corresponding stress on the idea of duty implies at the same time that religion, as conceived by Luther, is not a derivative or composite of other drives. Its distinguishing mark is precisely its simplicity, its immediacy of feeling, its emotional straightforwardness. Naturally, religion can be dissolved in the way Simmel has attempted to dissolve it, just as a "more deeply probing psychology" can dissolve the ethical into the eudaemonistic. But no one actually committed to religion is likely to recognize his own religion in such a portrayal. . . .

40. It is the merit of Nathan Soederblom and Rudolf Otto that they have established the significance of this concept for religion. However, they do not emphasize the distinctiveness of Luther's view sufficiently strongly.

in us. This sensation always means that we become aware of a higher reality that tears us loose from our ordinary existence and world-view. The Holy obtrudes upon us as something far above common experience, something that seeks to draw us up to itself and yet at once sets up limits if we rashly approach too closely.

In Luther, the idea of the Holy was deepened by the Christian idea of the Creator, and even more by the fact that it was closely, even exclusively, related to conscience. Hence we do not encounter the Holy merely on the low level of a kind of accidental confrontation within a world that exists independently of this higher reality. The Holy is personal will that commands reverence. From the outset we are under obligation, and we continue to be bound to the God who has appeared to us in this way. For we are beholden to him for our being and for all the blessings of life. The fact that this same God now confronts us as the Holy One suggests a higher order of reality which God desires to establish beyond the level of mere creation, compared with which the "world" is only transitory and temporal. Luther elucidated the meaning of this order through his interpretation of love to God and one's neighbor, and thus gave new force to the idea of the Holy. He stripped off everything in the nature of a taboo which the Catholic church had attached to it; he broke with the belief that the Holy is something tangible that adheres to certain objects, garments, vessels, and locations like a magical power. The Holy with which God actually lays hold of us is that noble idea of a true community with God and with one another which is expressed in the gospel. God, however, desires this supreme goal so emphatically and with such determination that in his wrath he annihilates everything that arises to oppose it.

Understood in this sense, the Holy becomes all the more a power that jolts us out of our comfortable equilibrium. It becomes something terrifying and oppressive, an unbearable judgment: as if God wanted to consume—Luther even says to devour—us: "At first his greeting is frightful . . . , as when lightning strikes a tree or a man."[41] For now the Holy forces us to consider whether we

41. *WA* 7, p. 365, l. 5. . . .

have any right to be in the higher order, or whether we belong to the transitory order that God annihilates. The tremendous reality that here ārises before us renders our whole personal existence uncertain.

More superficial feelings, such as wonder at the grandeur of God, cannot even arise alongside this feeling of judgment. When it is a matter of life or death there is no room for perception of the beauty of the world or for Dionysian ecstasy over the sublime, from whose presence one would rather vanish in shame.[42] The whole world, along with God, will inevitably seem antagonistic to us. And this is how we should feel. Luther from the outset questioned the religious sincerity of anyone who has never trembled to the depth of his soul in the presence of God. This is why he could dispose of the Zwickau prophets so quickly. People who have really been confronted by God have a different appearance, Luther thought, and do not speak about God as those conceited fellows who genially put themselves on such intimate terms with him.[43]

Fear of God is therefore the first step toward religion; note well, *toward* religion, for fear in itself is not yet religion. Real religion for Luther begins only when a person is united with God. As long as fear alone is in control, all service of God is hypocrisy, indeed mockery of God, for the heart is still far from him. We necessarily hate someone who frightens and judges us, no matter how much we may desire to have God on our side.

But is it possible to proceed from fear of God to consciousness of community with him without losing the seriousness of that fundamental experience? Mysticism had offered a simple solution that seems very plausible today. Its answer comes to this, that we possess an indestructible bridge to God in the depth of our own soul. We can mount it as often as we please, simply by remembering that our origin is in God. Even guilt is no barrier. By leaving behind our feeling of selfhood we also get rid of our sin.

---

42. I should like to emphasize particularly that Luther's sense of the Holy is also free from all "Dionysian" feelings.

43. Enders 3, p. 271. He speaks even more harshly elsewhere: "We have prophets everywhere who teach the people an all-too-easy boldness and who speak to the divine majesty as to a cobbler's boy" (*WA* 12, p. 499, l. 15).

Luther could never understand this line of thought. It represented a side of mysticism which even during the period of its greatest influence had escaped him completely. When he later found similar ideas among the Radicals, he opposed them vehemently. It was inconceivable to him how anyone could so quickly surmount his conscience, how one could fail to see that the question of guilt is paramount. Luther was not able to transcend the self because his sense of responsibility made him hold on to the consciousness of his selfhood. What he had done, he, this identical Martin Luther, had done. To deny or weaken this most simple and certain fact to him meant fleeing from reality into a world of fantasy.

Here really is the nerve center of Luther's whole view; this is the point where his religion most clearly shows itself to be a religion of conscience. In analyzing this question, Luther could only admonish the individual to stop short in his sense of terror before God and to attain clarity about the mind of God and his deeper purposes. By requiring this deepening of the self and by indicating more nearly the direction it should take, Luther also shed strikingly new light upon the realities of the life of the soul generally.

One of Luther's earliest insights was the recognition that there is no part of the soul that is static, as both the Scholastics and the mystics had assumed. As surely as the soul is a living thing, so surely is it constantly and totally in motion, whether it be in love or in hate. Behind this ceaseless movement, however, and giving rise to it—and this is the second significant insight—stands a desiring will, a self-will that seeks to assert itself in the surrounding world and evaluates everything with which it comes in contact in terms of personal advantage. With these statements Luther made the same advance in his doctrine of the soul that he had made in his concept of God and his view of the world—all spiritual life, in fact all of life generally, is motion, activity, and ultimately will. From here he arrived at a conclusion regarding the ultimate quality of human nature exactly opposite that of the mystics. The mystics asserted that the "ground" of the soul is something independent of the self, penetrating beyond individual existence into the infinite. By staying close to realities, Luther discovered that the real ground of the soul is the sense of selfhood, a tenacious selfishness, straitening or constricting it to the self. At no moment do we will anything other than ourselves; we are compelled by a natural constraint to do this. This is what we dimly perceive when we are terrified by God's holiness. It dawns upon us that we always instinctively want something different from our prescribed duty, something other than what we are commanded to will, for to will ourselves and the will to serve God are irreconcilable opposites.

Luther did not forget that there is in us also something nobler, a spirit, an original aspiration after God, a desire for pure goodness, what the Middle Ages called the *syntheresis.* How could he, who based his whole religion on conscience, have failed to take this into account? The fact that we become aware of the wrongness of our own egotism presupposes, as Luther well knew, the impulse and the awareness of this higher element. But Luther refused to regard this higher element as a sphere untouched by the other impulses of the soul; this would be to dissect a person in Scholastic fashion into individual "parts." But a person is really a living unity, totally present in every impulse and action. The sensual nature (the "flesh") belongs to the same being as the spirit. Coarse and refined elements not only coexist but permeate each other. The nobler, "better" self never exists apart from the influence of the flesh upon it. To estimate our own real worth, our value in God's sight, we must not indulgently repress the embarrassing aspects of our being but must see ourselves as one whole, undivided person.

Following Paul, however, Luther added the further observation that in the inevitable conflict between these lower and higher forces, self-will (or concupiscence, as he also called it) is actually always dominant. For self-will is always first on the scene; indeed, it is an integral part of the activity of the will itself; and it is stronger than the desire for nobler things because it remains largely unconscious. Secretly, stealthily, egotism is always able to insinuate itself and to pervert even that which has been well begun. Not only in yielding to natural inclination but especially in trying to do better, in the effort to serve only God and the neighbor, does the drive for self-preservation quietly intrude itself into the actual determination of the will. It may do so crassly, as when persistent desires are suppressed through fear of punishment, or more subtly, as when the eudaemonistic hope for beatitude or rest in God secretly tips the scales in favor of the nobler aspiration. Yet Luther strongly insisted that this secret determining factor is a real will. It is not, as the Scholastics thought, simply a matter of concurrently competing ideas, of stimuli that affect us only casually and can, therefore, be overlooked in self-examination; it is not merely a question of the aftereffects of the so-called tinder of sin [*fomes peccati*] for which we are only partly responsible. Rather, it is a matter of impulses issuing from the depths of our being, of forces continually active in us, manifestations of a definitely directed aspiration that seeks to control the whole person. This recognition of the existence of an unconscious will was in itself a real breakthrough; what was even more significant, however, was that Luther demanded that a person should take full responsibility even for this unconscious will.

This more profound insight forced Luther to reject as inadequate the remedy traditionally offered by philosophy when faced with this problem; namely, to rouse the will and to generate a noble passion by calling to mind the moral law that lifts us above ourself. He had to insist that this solution fails at the crucial point. The same reaction takes place when the heart is confronted by the law's clear command as when the instinctive higher aspirations try to assert themselves. No law can liberate us from ourselves. The law actually produces hypocrites. For the constraint of law always gives rise to a spontaneous opposition that can only be suppressed by force—and thus proves itself to be the true human will. Even when the law is freely affirmed out of sincere enthusiasm, regard for one's own dignity and the enhancement of one's own personality is always present—and the ego accordingly remains dominant. Close analysis shows that this kind of effort is actually nothing more than refined self-love. Luther saw this long before Kant raised this fatal objection to his own ethic.

Now Luther has arrived at a point that would seem to frustrate the whole purpose of his exposition. If it is really impossible for us in this life to get rid of the selfishness that clings to us like our shadow, then in what sense can this self-will be guilt? As a natural drive, is it not rather a fate, a misfortune that we must endure, a painful burden we can bear but which we cannot without affectation regard as guilt? Luther faced this question squarely. He appraised and answered it in his doctrine of original sin, for by original sin he meant that very same egotistical self-will. But having so designated it, he also felt bound to show at what point the sense of responsibility for one's inborn nature must come in.

Luther readily conceded that if original sin were only something inherited, only a power that coerces a person, there could be no question of personal responsibility. How could we feel guilty for something we have not actually done? In regard to particular acts, however, we can never claim that we had no alternative to wrong-doing. Even though we may regularly succumb, we still feel that we should have, and therefore also could have, done differently. The truth is that we never succumb without assenting to the wrong. The various gradations connected with this, from the heedless plunge into carnal pleasure to reluctant submission to a deceptive power, prove that the power to resist is present in us, and that the demand to resist evil, which is inherent in the moral sense, is in no way absurd.

Luther's thinking, however, went even deeper. Human nature must not be thought of as merely an unfortunate but fated inheritance from Adam. Awareness that a person is a living and active whole helps us to see that there is a continual re-creation of the ethical nature, of the very self, on the part of the person. We have not become what we are at any given instant without our own will. If evil passions and instincts stir in us, we are at fault for not having previously guarded against them and for not having already reeducated ourselves. In this sense, one is still one's own image, one's own act in every part of one's being, even though this being was inherited from Adam. Ultimately, the reason we are what we are lies in our egos, our affirmation of ourselves. Luther intends to express this profound idea when he calls original sin "personal sin" [*Personsünde*].[44]

44. E.g., *WA* 10¹, p. 508, l. 20.

Luther actually touched the heart of the question here. He was confronting the individual with an ultimate, decisive choice, a clear question of either/or. Either we are responsible for nothing, or we are responsible for ourself as one whole. We can deny responsibility for any act because we can always represent it as the result of involuntary forces within ourself. But by doing so, we relinquish the great gift God has given us in the consciousness of duty, along with the promise of liberation from inner constraint implied in it. If, however, we choose the alternative, we must remember the extent of our responsibility, which includes not only the specific deed but also all the inner motives behind it, indeed our whole inner being. To perceive this and to see oneself enslaved to self-seeking can only lead to the feeling that before God one is absolutely guilty, that one's whole person is completely reprehensible in the sight of God. It is to Luther's great credit that he dared to think this through and to take his stand upon it. This is why he rightly regarded his doctrine of original sin as an integral part of his outlook, which he could not afford to tone down.[45] All the strength of his sense of responsibility asserted itself at this point. By taking this stand he subscribed to the axiom: the greater the responsibility, the more authentic the existence.[46]

This proves that Luther's doctrine of original sin did not issue

---

45. For this reason Luther opposed not only Scholasticism's weak doctrine of original sin but also Augustine's (*WA* 8, p. 89, ll. 23ff.) and Zwingli's (Enders 5, p. 262, l. 11; *WA* 20, p. 621, l. 8).

46. Th. Häring, in an article that illuminates every aspect of the question (*ZThK,* 1922, pp. 237ff.), has thoroughly taken issue with Luther on this point. Despite his agreement with Luther on other points, he finds it intolerable that we should be expected to impute to ourself as personal guilt something we have inherited. By distinguishing sinfulness [*Sündhaftigkeit*] and personal guilt, he hopes to effect a correction of Luther's view. While even something inherited can be sinful, i.e., reprehensible in God's sight, there can be no guilt unless there was a real possibility to affirm or reject the will of God that seeks to win us. I do not believe that this really constitutes an improvement. I would address two questions to Häring: (1) On what basis does he label something inherited as sinful if the personal will is not involved? Would it not be something purely material, something morally indeterminate? Or if he is referring to inherited negative character traits, is it possible to make a judgment that is equally valid for every human being? (2) Where is the boundary between what is inherited and what is truly one's own? Who can draw this line with respect to oneself? And who can determine the point in time when one's own will first became operative? Both objections would seem to require the conclusion drawn by Luther.

from a desire to become guilty before God at all costs. To a certain extent, this charge may be made against monasticism and mysticism. The fostering of the sense of sin was not devoid here of a secret feeling of self-gratification. Luther, on the other hand, always regarded the sense of guilt as pure agony. When he nevertheless decided to push his doctrine of original sin to the most extreme point, he did so only because he had come to see matters in this way and felt constrained so to see them.

For everything that has been said so far was more to Luther than a contrived theory; it was something he experienced again and again and with great intensity of feeling,[47] namely, whenever he was beset by *Anfechtungen*. Up to now, these experiences of his have not received the attention they deserve, even though Luther frequently referred to their importance for his inner life. Because they always led him to the most profound depths he was in a certain sense proud of them, despite the terrors they brought. In all modesty, he felt akin to the great figures of religion because of them. He thought that Paul and the prophets must have had such temptations, too, else they would not have been able to write their books. These experiences actually played the same role in his life, as, for example, visions do in the mystic's. In these temptations God himself confronted Luther directly as a reality, as the Holy One. Because of his very acute sense of sin, this kind of experience of God proved to be much more shattering to him than the similar experiences of the German mystics. Luther's *Anfechtungen* were not, to use Tauler's expression, merely a winter of godforsakenness: they were an assault of God upon him, an attack that threatened to destroy him. At each occurrence the same basic question confronted him. Is it possible in face of an absolute self-condemnation to attain the consciousness of being one with God? He never came to a point where the sense of sin turned of itself into a consciousness of grace. In contrast to the German mystics, Luther needed a clear, objective basis for daring to ap-

---

47. The "feeling" (*sentire*) is essential in this connection. See *WA* 40¹, p. 73, l. 10, and p. 74, l. 2: "the sin which the conscience feels . . . ," "words are easy, but to feel that grace, apart from everything else . . . remits sin [is difficult]." Drews, *Disputationen*, p. 211: ". . . when God touches us and enters into judgment with us."

proach God whenever this situation recurred. Each time he had to recover anew, and through great pains, the truth that had on previous occasions brought deliverance.

Two things need to be pointed out here. The first is that these *Anfechtungen* always took Luther by surprise. This confirms his view that genuine religion originates in an experience of the divine that is neither sought nor desired. Suddenly, unexpectedly, in the stillness of the night the Numinous is there! It does not appear that any special sin that weighed heavily upon him the previous day was the occasion for it. Frequently Satan reproached him with events of times past, such as that for fifteen years he had blasphemed God by celebrating the Mass. But his anguish came from the fact that suddenly, while recalling individual deeds, the supreme and absolute standard would strike him and a total awareness of his worth—or rather of his unworthiness—before God would emerge. In a flash he saw how far he was from the goal he should have attained in all things. This fact, in addition to the terrible fear he experienced, kept him from even thinking of contriving a procedure to produce such experiences artificially—as the mystics and even A. H. Francke did. It was entirely for God to determine whether and how he would confront the individual with the ultimate experience. Only then could the event be taken seriously. Nor did Luther at this point forget that there is a difference between "strong" and "weak" Christians. How little inclined he was to push others into such straits without good reason can be seen in the fact that he felt his only duty toward those in *Anfechtung* was to bring comfort.

Secondly, it is worth noting how in his thinking about *Anfechtung* Luther intermingled God and the devil; but he was in no danger, as has often been assumed, of confusing good and evil. It was the very clear voice of conscience[48] that produced his anguish. Yet he was uncertain about the ultimate meaning of the *Anfechtung,* whether it was only a temptation or a real judgment. At first he thought it was the former, and therefore regarded Satan as the power that seized him. For since he had experienced

---

48. See *WA* 40¹, p. 73, l. 2: "our two devils: sin and conscience; 'the power of the law, afterwards [I found to be] the stimulus of sin.' "

peace with God and considered it his duty to rely on him at all times, it could be no one but Satan who tried to sever him from God and plunge him into despair and even into hatred of God. Once he saw this as Satan's design, the battle was soon over. The *Anfechtung* now was merely an occasion to emphasize the completely gracious character of his relationship to God. He could mockingly reply to Satan that he did not claim to be the saint he ought to be, that he knew full well what a sinner he was and therefore relied solely upon God's mercy and Christ's atonement.

The *Anfechtung* could, however, be more serious, especially when a rebuke administered by his conscience cut so deep that he saw it to be a well-deserved judgment on his whole being. Then he saw that his attacker was not Satan but God, and now he really experienced God's wrath against himself. These were the periods when the new meaning of Christ that had begun to dawn on him first became completely clear to him. Now he saw Christ not merely as the one who, in the past, had once for all placated God's wrath, but as the one who even now was interceding effectually in his behalf. He perceived how a power flowed into him from Christ's death and resurrection which gave him both the assurance of pardon and the confidence to defeat the power of the sin that still clung to him.[49]

49. Luther went beyond the Catholic conception of the work of Christ at two points. (1) He regarded the death of Christ strictly as punishment borne by him vicariously for humanity. We must not allow ourselves to be misled by Luther's use of the Catholic terms "satisfaction" and "merit," for he uses them in a different sense. In the Catholic view, *satisfactio* means the rendering of substitutionary compensation for damages to God. Thus Anselm could formulate an "either-or": *aut satisfactio aut poena*. Anselm regarded the latter alternative as impossible. Luther, on the contrary, finds precisely in *poena* the true meaning of Christ's death, which is obviously connected with his more severe understanding of God and sin. Sin can never be made good, and God is not one who can be bought off. The only possible satisfaction to be given for the transgression of his law, which angers him, is the enduring of punishment. Catholic dogmaticians then and now refuse to accept this idea. But Luther has thought it through to the end, in connection with Christ's cry, "My God, my God, why hast thou forsaken me?" On the cross Christ really experienced the wrath of God (*WA* 40¹, p. 449, ll. 1ff.). . . . (2) In Luther's thinking, the death of Christ is intimately connected with his resurrection. "His resurrection from the dead is our justification through faith alone" (Drews, *Disputationen,* p. 732, thesis 2). Here Luther counteracts the one-sidedness characteristic of Western theology since the time of Anselm, which also overtook later Lutheran theology under Melanchthon's influence—namely, the idea that the death of Christ is the one great fact of salvation. Luther

Sometimes it even happened that Christ himself seemed to vanish or that Satan, as Luther put it, appeared in the guise of

---

revives the Pauline view that death and resurrection constitute an inseparable unity. It is most significant for him that the death of Christ, which is the execution of the judgment of wrath, is not God's last word. Christ's death is rather "that strange battle between life and death, where life emerged victorious by swallowing up death." For this favorite expression of Luther's, see also *WA* 40¹, p. 439, ll. 10ff.; p. 440, ll. 3ff. . . . Because of the resurrection we are able to see through the judgment of wrath into God's grace, into the *benedictio,* as Luther says in the passage last cited. But he associated with the resurrection (and again Paul is his source) the further thought that Christ as spirit can now be present in the believer. Christ did not ascend to heaven, according to Luther, to vindicate his own honor but in order to become the more active in and through people. This "Christ-mysticism," as it is now called, belongs to the first portion of the Pauline heritage to come alive in Luther, in whom it attained a vitality greater than in medieval mysticism (*WA* 3, p. 433, l. 2). . . . Christ is present *in* the true believer (*WA* 40¹, p. 233, l. 3; p. 229, l. 4) . . . not as object of the believer's delight or manipulation, as was frequently the case among the mystics, but as source of power in the struggle against sin. The Christ who was resurrected in his own person is resurrected again in the believer (Drews, *Disputationen,* p. 424, thesis 37). . . . So Christ comes to the believer daily (*WA* 40¹, p. 16, l. 27) . . . and as Lord of Hosts carries on his warfare in the believer (*WA* 30², p. 621, l. 17). . . .

The strengthening the believer experiences through clinging to Christ is twofold. First, by recognizing (in faith) the meaning of Christ's death as the stilling of God's wrath, one is assured of the forgiveness of sins. Secondly, if one's faith is more than mere assent to historical propositions one also receives the assurance that the sin that yet accuses one can be conquered through the power of Christ (Drews, *Disputationen,* p. 37, thesis 35; p. 10, thesis 12 . . .). To put it differently, Luther regards faith as a coming to grips not only with the guilt of sin but also with its power. This is essential. Only because he can trust in a divine power that purges him of sin does Luther have a "clear conscience," and sin, death, and the devil are really vanquished for him. We see here how unjust it is to regard Luther's faith as mere "comfort in the misery of sin" and on this basis to give an advantage to Calvin. The slogan of mere "comfort in the misery of sin" applies only to Lutheran Orthodoxy (influenced by Melanchthon), not to Luther himself. The attempt of the later Orthodoxy (and of Pietism as well) to remedy this obvious weakness by insisting that faith must be accompanied by the resolve not to sin again indicates all the more clearly the distance between these views and Luther's. According to Luther, we receive strength for the future not from our own resolve to do better but from reliance upon the power of God and Christ, to whom we feel the more deeply bound by the forgiveness we have received.

The starting points of Luther's conception of the person and work of Christ are thus clear and understandable. They sustain a firm relation to the innermost impulses of his piety. It is therefore completely wrong to regard Luther's Christology as merely the consequence of his doctrine of the Lord's Supper; the decisive points of his Christology are laid down before the beginning of the eucharistic controversy. But Luther is now at the same time convinced that his conception merely expresses the true meaning of the ancient dogma. . . . In this respect he was mistaken. Luther did not simply receive the ancient dogma, but he developed it, and in such a way that, from the standpoint of the ancient councils, he skirted the borders of heresy all along the line.

Christ.[50] For Christ was certainly also God. He was lawgiver and judge, although he was more than this, too. How then could he help Luther against "God"? The fact that sometimes Christ seemed to recede in this way is significant. It confirms what was

---

In Christology Luther regarded it as an essential point that the divinity of Christ is revealed in his very humanity. . . . To learn the true will of God, one must keep to the humanity of Christ. This was something different from, and something more serious than, say, the mysticism of Saint Bernard, in which the religious relationship begins with sensitivity and sympathy for the one who is being abused, and where the compassionate onlooker suddenly remembers that the sufferer is moreover also God. Luther insists that the divine, the will of God, be intuited quite directly in the apparently human acts and sufferings of Christ. . . . What matters is the unity [of the two natures]. . . . But when Luther sought to express his view in the ancient two-nature terminology, he came close to monophysitism. In this respect Schwenckfeld, from whose views Luther diligently sought to distinguish his own, merely drew the ultimate conclusion from his position.

With respect to the doctrine of the Trinity the situation was very similar. Luther regarded it as a point not to be yielded that the activity of Christ was the very activity of God, that the will of Christ was not only in full accord with the will of God but even identical with it. Therefore Christ had to be essentially God. In this sense Luther even defended the application of such titles as "Lord Zabaoth" and "Jehovah" to Christ. . . . A theologian of the ancient church, even Augustine, would never have drawn these conclusions, but would have regarded them as improper. Concerning the famous *quaestio* of Peter Lombard, he affirmed: "The essence begets when it is taken in a personal sense (*essentia generat cum capitur personaliter*)" (Drews, *Disputationen,* pp. 788, 808, 861, 869). Luther's fundamental concern in all this was to understand the unity of the Godhead as vital and personal. But if he thus approached modalism, he inferred at the same time (and unintentionally) a subordination of the Son to the Father. For Christ was also always for him the "gift of God" to humanity, the instrument employed by God—see his constantly repeated formula, "gift and example." This subordination is extended even to the deity of Christ: Christ has received his deity from the Father (Drews, *Disputationen,* pp. 516, 518 . . .). Therefore he leads people not to himself but to the Father; he does not his own will but the will of the Father. Such a doctrine accords well enough with Paul and John, but poorly with the Nicene dogma. The distance between Luther and Nicaea is increased by his assumption that, in line with 1 Corinthians 15:24, the work of Christ (and of the Holy Spirit) will cease in eternity. . . . One would like to ask Luther what becomes of the humanity of Christ when Christ has completed his work and has given back his dominion to the Father.

The fault in all this lies with the ancient dogma, not with Luther. A piety centered upon the will and a community of will was bound to collide everywhere with concepts like "substance" and "nature"—derived from the ancient *natural* metaphysics, and regarded as abiding entities of purely ontological determinateness—and with the correspondingly shallow conception of the person.

50. It is of course only a literary device when Luther often pretends that only those standing on a higher level (e.g., Tauler) are deemed worthy of this type of *Anfechtung*. His description shows that he is speaking from his own experience. Baptism and the Lord's Supper now utterly failed, too, to provide the support they normally gave to his faith.

said above, namely, that contrary to common opinion, Luther's piety was not Christ-centered in the sense that his whole faith was based totally and solely on Christ. Moreover, we must recall that Luther never regarded this "forgetting of Christ" as sin or as unfaithfulness to him but as a trial imposed by God himself. Thus there really were times when he felt himself to be facing God directly and alone. Only at this level does his most profound piety emerge, and only here do we see clearly how he was able to advance from fear of God to union with him.

What sustained Luther in such moments of extreme crisis was something surprisingly simple, the First Commandment. In his mortal need he always clung to its opening words, "I am the Lord thy God." Nowhere is it so obvious as here that the feeling of obligation forms the basis of his whole piety and that obligation to God is the most basic of all duties. His final resort was to a commandment—the very one that was judging him. For the First Commandment sums up all duty to God, the duty of which he had been neglectful—for all his sin was self-seeking, and therefore ultimately unbelief and ingratitude. He laid hold of this commandment in order earnestly to affirm both the commandment and its judgment upon himself. He would not allow himself or anyone else to have recourse to any thoughts that might becloud the purity of the moral struggle, such as the desire to get rid of his fear, or the hope that the *Anfechtung* might diminish of itself, or a feeling of hatred toward an unmerciful God which might result in a convenient despair. Instead, the wrath of God must be bravely not defiantly endured, but in such a way that God's judgment of condemnation—and, consequently, God himself—is recognized as completely just.

The more earnestly Luther determined to do this, the more clearly he heard the word of comfort contained in the same commandment. Just as his sense of unworthiness had driven him to the verge of despair and he felt ready to sink into the ground before God, the continuing obligation of the commandment came into clear focus in his mind. We must always obey God, always; and that means even when it seems impossible to do so; even now, in this very situation. When a commandment becomes difficult, the time has come to obey it. If he tried to avoid the command now, he would add a new and more grievous sin to his burden. And yet, to obey the First Commandment's mandate to "have God as one's God" at a time like this also meant to believe that in spite of his judgment God, for his part, was continuing to maintain the community relationship. Although God wants to crush the guilty through judgment, he intends to let them live before him. This implies the hope of forgiveness; for one cannot live before him unless one's sins are forgiven. Thus Luther was able to peer through the gloom and fury of the divine wrath into the loving will of God. As he wonderfully expressed it, he now hears "below and above the 'Nay' the deep and hidden 'Yea' " which God was speaking to him.

This description of the process of justification, which Luther was actually portraying here, makes very evident how completely he rejected the idea that it is merely our instinct for self-preservation (which cannot and will not accept the fact that we deserve to be destroyed) which here asserts itself to make us throw ourselves into the arms of a God who saves us. Anyone who approaches God in this way has no solid basis for claiming justification. The assurance that he may stand before God despite his sin Luther found in the very will of God which opposed him during this struggle, rather than in his own invincible will to live. By reference to his own experience he showed how awareness of a never-ending belonging-to-God begins to arise out of the tempted person's awareness of an unceasing obligation to him. As God's command closed in upon him he began to see that there was no way out of his relationship to God. Even if he should have to bear the punishment for his sin, he would not be relieved of the duty to obey God. The commandment to have God as his own personal God would apply to him even in hell. In this way Luther battled his way through each crisis to arrive at the greatest conceptual strictness. He consistently regarded his relationship to God as one of pure duty with unlimited implications. But then this same relationship to God, conceived strictly in terms of duty, became the firm ground under his feet. The fact that God even now confronted him with a commandment, with this particular commandment, was proof that God had not forsaken him but was actually on his side! By keeping the First Commandment in force, even after rejecting him, God in a sense called him again into his service. This will of God appeared as something new and unexpected, because the full severity of the previous judgment was in no way removed. In fact, it was so far from being removed that faith could recognize the love of God that seeks us precisely in the relentless integrity with which God holds us under judgment. It was God's intention thus to cure us of our self-will. Only by seeing ourself in this light do we know that God forgives us.[51] The expression "by faith alone" [*sola fide*] simply describes most appropriately the only fitting attitude on our part toward such grace.

Surely it has now become clear that to Luther justification was anything but a mere rational deduction, say, from the reality of the moral law. Luther insists that faith in the forgiveness of sins goes "against all reason,"[52] in fact, against all "morality." He even uses such extreme expressions as that one here acts "against one's own conscience" to overcome "God with God." According to Luther, "reason" and "conscience" can understand God in no other way than as recognizing the one who acts justly in his sight. The teaching of the gospel, that God is interested in the sinner, must seem absurd and destructive of all morality. Luther goes even further by saying that God himself takes this point of view. His law is the serious expression of his will. And yet the gospel is

---

51. To spell this out further—God can put away his wrath as soon as he has brought us to the point where we can see ourselves as we are and are fully aware of the conflict between God's will and our natural self-assertiveness. See *WA* 5, p. 206, ll. 18ff. . . . From the human side, justification would be the moment when we attain the courage to regard *Anfechtung* itself as a gift from God.

52. All of Luther's harsh words about "reason" have their point of departure here. It is "practical reason" that he has primarily in mind. . . . See *WA* 17¹, p. 431, l. 2: "Reason may indeed acknowledge God as an awful, wrathful judge. . . . But nature can never sincerely call him Father." A somewhat different thought is found in *WA* 19, p. 206, ll. 12ff.: "The natural light of reason is sufficient to regard God as good, gracious, compassionate, mild . . . but it cannot believe that God is really willing and desirous to act that way . . . it knows and believes that he is able to, but doubts that he wants to, because the misfortunes of life seem to prove the opposite." . . .

true; in fact, it is *the* truth about God. Thus Luther makes the "foolishness" of the gospel more perceptible than anyone in the church had done since Paul.[53] We ought to believe with all sincerity that we encounter God himself in the *Anfechtung*; for conscience' sake, we ought to believe that judgment upon us is God's last word. And yet we ought also to believe that judgment upon us is not the last word, and that the God who confronts us in righteous wrath is not, after all, the "real" God.

Faith in forgiveness now becomes a great venture, an audacity, devotion to an improbability, an affirmation of something that has no basis in experience at the expense of something that very definitely and distinctly has been experienced.[54] Nevertheless, the leap of faith is not taken in a defiant mood or in a rash skipping-over of all barriers. Nor is faith adopted merely as a "postulate." It is approached from a sense of obligation, in humble obedience. The required courage comes ultimately from the feeling that through such confidence in God we render him the supreme honor that we unquestionably *owe* him. Only the person who thinks well of God thinks rightly of him; this is the inner motive. Only that conscience is well ordered which is fully convinced of the love of God.[55] To deny that the God who reveals himself in *Anfechtung* is capable of good is to blaspheme God to his face, for that is tantamount to denying that he is God. We have the *right* to subdue our own selves, our "consciences," and the picture of God that confronts us in judgment, because we *ought* to believe in

53. Luther was even more aware than Paul of the dangers inherent in the doctrine of justification. "The forgiveness of sins should make thee joyful —this is the chief point of Christian doctrine and yet most dangerous preaching" (*WA* 27, p. 378, l. 9). . . .

54. See *WA* 10³, p. 239, l. 13: "For this is the nature of faith, that it presumes on God's grace and creates good favor and confidence toward him. . . . Faith does not require information, knowledge, or certitude, but a joyful daring and a free surrender to his unfelt, untried, unproved goodness." *WA* 15, p. 536, l. 32: "where therefore the word becomes powerful, it follows that we confide in God, however much we may be in disgrace, death, and sin. God is not to be known through feeling but through faith."

55. Besides the oft-repeated sentence "As your conscience is, so is your God," this rule holds too (*WA* 20, 236, ll. 13ff.): "if it portrays God as judge, a judge he is; if as a father, so he is; if as Satan, so he is. If I regard him as a shopkeeper, so he is; not because he is so by nature, but because he is so by my nature and conscience. No conscience is right unless it regards God as merciful, who freely (*gratis*) bestows his grace and mercy; such a conscience is right and holds together."

the God who is well disposed toward us.[56] It is not a matter of reasoning from a general principle, namely God's goodness, to a specific situation. If we find faith in the course of an *Anfechtung* it is because we believe not in a timeless truth but in the will of God confronting us at that very moment; yet it is not the wrathful will that judges us, but rather its opposite, which we intuit directly as the true will of God concealed beneath the wrath.

From this ultimate perspective the apparent contradiction in the "justification of the sinner" is resolved. God very properly regards as "righteous" anyone who renders him the highest possible honor by acknowledging his unmerited goodness. But Luther insisted that this approach be followed all the way. Anyone who risks such a faith must assume the entire risk. The mood that Catholicism always produced—and we find traces of this even amidst the exuberance of mysticism—was to entrust oneself to God only timidly and intermittently, with some misgivings.[57] To Luther this is a false humility. It is much more appropriate to take a grand view of God, for all that he does and gives is grand. God is not honored but insulted when one places only a slight confidence in him—"as if some emperor desired to give a beggar a grand imperial gift and the fool asked for nothing more than a bowl of soup." God is no shopkeeper desirous of haggling with us. He gives on his own initiative and does not bestow his grace piecemeal. Whatever he does, he does entirely, and he does it all at once. The "Yea" he speaks to us in forgiveness is a complete Yea. Therefore no halfway position is possible for us, either. We can only feel ourselves to be under God's wrath or grace. If we decide to believe in forgiveness at all, we must also take the next step and trust that everything has now really been cleared up between ourself and God.

Thus for Luther, too, faith culminates in the consciousness of being completely at one with God. But this union has nothing to

---

56. See the characteristic expression (*WA* 16, p. 65, ll. 8ff.): "We should take note of this in death: "I have the word that I ought to live, and yet death oppresses me. We should always cling to the first promise, 'Thou shalt live'; then say: 'Death here, death there, the Lord has promised me that I ought to live; this I believe.' "

57. See proceedings of the Council of Trent on penance, session 14, ch. 3.

do with the soul's absorption sought by the mystics. It is most significant and again shows the gradation Luther maintained between God and Christ (in defiance of dogma) that whereas he often affirmed that the believer becomes "one loaf" with Christ, he never used this expression for the relationship to God.[58] No less significant is the fact that Luther never used the term "friendship" to describe the divine-human relationship—a usage originated by Augustine[59] and developed by the Scholastics. At every point he wants to preserve the distance between human beings and God. The union attained is only a union of will; an "affective" union, as Luther put it, not a "substantial" union. The emphasis on forgiveness, too, wards off a familiarity that might venture to put human beings on equal terms with God. A purity in the religious relationship is thus maintained which was not possible within mysticism.

Now this certitude with respect to God results in a most unique development of the religious self-awareness, indeed of self-awareness as such. At this point Luther, too, is confronted by the question of the meaning of the self in religion. But his answer differs from that of the mystics. For him, the self is not absorbed; it is preserved as consciousness and will, but seems at the same time to be yoked to the paradox inherent in the meaning of forgiveness. For forgiveness, according to Luther, does not mean that the memory of past sin is simply wiped out. Like Paul, rather, he believes that true repentance arises only after forgiveness, because only then do we comprehend against what kind of God, against how benevolent a God, we have sinned. Thus the relation to the "self" that committed the sin is maintained. But this forgiveness also gives us the right inwardly to detach ourselves from this self. This forgiveness creates a new self and fills it with

---

58. Lutheran Orthodoxy's doctrine of the mystical union is accordingly not a faithful representation of Luther's own thought. Orthodoxy asserts a mystical union with the triune God which it describes as *unio substantiarum* but not as *unio substantialis* or *personalis*. Yet Luther vigorously asserted the latter type of union (see *WA* 50¹, p. 285, ll. 5ff.)—only with Christ, however, not with God. This again shows how faithfully Luther follows Paul who also taught only a Christ-mysticism, but no God-mysticism.

59. See "Augustins innere Entwicklung" [Augustine's inner development], *GA* 3, p. 86.

a high self-awareness that contrasts sharply with the former, which rested on a natural consciousness of strength. Those who are reconciled to God may say to themselves that although they are nothing and unworthy of God, yet God has raised them up and regarded them as worthy of perpetual community with himself. This means that they have been accorded a new honor, the highest honor, the only true honor. Luther even wants to emphasize this new sort of self-awareness. We not only may, but like Paul we are expected to, glory in the grace we have received. This is a part of the gratitude we owe to God, and it is at the same time the proof of our own assurance. Further, the more we become conscious of the magnitude of what has been given us, the more surely are we inwardly transformed by it. For whoever experiences the meaning of the new relationship to God finds that new standards of value, new affections, new powers of the will arise from it. It is impossible to know oneself to be at one with God without at the same time affirming his will as alone valid. One cannot sincerely thank God without at the same time experiencing the impulse to do his will freely, joyfully, and with inner delight. What produces this human renewal is not, as the Scholastics imagined, a mysteriously infused power accompanying the forgiveness of sins. The forgiveness of sins itself, that is, the consciousness of being accepted by God, immediately directs the will toward God as soon as it is understood and appreciated.

Yet Luther sets a definite limit in two directions. In the first place, he emphasizes that not only community with God but also the whole sense of self-awareness which is based on it must always be regarded as a gift. The basis of the new self-awareness always remains outside ourselves and in God. Man's new exultation, therefore, not only can but must be conjoined to the feeling of deepest unworthiness. "Faith is our recognition that we are not worthy of living on the earth," and "the gifts that we receive from God are so great as to be stunning." Goethe's "I exist for wonder" is here expressed in an even deeper sense. Anyone at one with God will never cease to marvel at the degree of exultation that is allowed.

In the second place, Luther continues to insist that despite the distinction between the new and the old self the psychological unity of the person is not broken. Having been saved from ourself and thus to some extent standing outside ourself by virtue of our relationship to God, we are not thereby translated into a dream world, a fool's paradise. Luther does not end up with a double life, a split in the self, as the mystics often did. The regenerate person continues to be bound to the "natural," actual self. The power of the flesh continues to be experienced as it affects even the spirit. Not, of course, in the sense of surrendering to it; Luther infers from it, rather, a commitment to the continuing moral struggle and invokes as his most effective weapon the consciousness of power which flows from the relationship with God. With God on our side, we are more than conquerors of any hostile power. Or, expressed even more forcefully: in the person who has grasped Christ by faith, Christ himself goes to war—the same Christ who desires to mold those united to him into his own image —and his victory is certain. Thus the religious sense of selfhood attains its full stature precisely through its antithesis, which it perceives and conquers and turns into a sense of victory and mastery. Luther again dares to sound the Pauline note that had died out in Christianity long before. He again dares to boast of his faith, to know himself to be master of all things, and to look upon the world, sin, death, and the devil, in fact, everything that would subdue him, as subjected to him by the power of God. This is the highest sense of selfhood imaginable; but it is also a completely temperate, completely humble, one may even say, an absolutely selfless sense of selfhood.

6. Luther's Concept of Christian Passivity

Only on the basis of this assurance of "having a God"[60] arises what Luther regards as true religion. Proceeding from the concept of the divine monergism, it goes without saying that Luther empha-

---

60. I would like to stress that the expression "to have a God" was not coined by Luther. It is already found in Augustine—did he coin it? . . .

sizes the receptive aspect of religion, that is, the acceptance of the working of God and the entering into his purpose. This emphasis, together with the close relationship to God of which he is now conscious, leads to an attitude toward God which differs all along from that of the Catholic church. This becomes immediately evident in Luther's view of direct communication with God in prayer. Since he was sure that God approaches us with unlimited grace, he could never undertake to attain a higher status or greater grace by exerting some sort of influence upon God. To "have God" is to have the highest that can fall to a person's lot. It follows that our participation in the relationship with God should begin with gratitude. This postulate signified a revolution over against the whole prevailing piety. Above all, the sacrifice of the Mass, the most important element in the traditional worship service, was to be done away with. In the attempt to secure God's grace by means of a sacrifice, Luther could see nothing but a disregard of what was already vouchsafed by God—a relapse into the Old Testament or into paganism. On the same basis Luther also rejected the ascetic use of prayer to acquire merits, as well as the belief that God's favorites, the saints, by virtue of their special *parresia,* could obtain things from God which he would deny to others. There is no aristocracy of divine favorites (*philoi*). All Christians share equally the rights vouchsafed to them as believers and children of God.

Luther sees it as one of his most important tasks to impress upon the Christian that the giving of thanks is a real duty. He feels that conscious, express recognition and affirmation of God's gifts is the honor that God asks above all else; it is the act in which his desire for personal fellowship with human beings finds fulfillment. Thus prayer becomes also a commitment to God and his will.[61] Prayer, even thanksgiving, becomes a very serious matter

61. Luther's statements to the effect that he was unable to pray without at the same time cursing (which Denifle located and on which Grisar dwelled at length) are related to this point. For example, *WA* 30³, p. 479, l. 19ff.: "I cannot pray without cursing at the same time. If I say 'Hallowed be thy name' I must also say 'Cursed, damned, and shamed be the name of the papists and all those who blaspheme thy name.' If I say 'Thy kingdom come' I must also add 'Cursed, damned, and destroyed be the papacy and all earthly kingdoms that oppose thy kingdom.' . . . Indeed, I continually pray with heart and mouth in this fashion, and with me all who believe in Christ—and I also feel that this prayer is heard." According to Grisar

when understood in this sense. Luther liked to recall the old monastic saying that there is no harder work than prayer. True prayer demands an exertion of the will, and the concentration of thought upon a clear goal. Hence he reacts angrily against the thoughtless repetition of prescribed prayers, and he also becomes suspicious of those forms of prayer which in Catholicism are regarded as prayer's highest level. Luther evidently was not acquainted with the "interior prayer" that was especially popular with the Latin mystics. Had he stumbled upon it, he surely would have rejected it at once because of its goal of mystical fusion with God. However, he was acquainted with and had himself practiced a related type of prayer, which regarded the spoken words of the rosary or the breviary merely as a barrier to external distractions or a sedative for one's inner turmoil, while the real approach to God took place deep within the hushed heart, apart from the spoken words. Luther always deeply appreciated prayers which, like the Lord's Prayer, could lead gradually beyond the meaning of the words to absorption of the spirit with God, that is, to pure adoration. He continued to pray in this fashion all his life. But as soon as he had come to know himself, he recognized in that other "mystical" prayer merely an aberration. Prayer must always remain a real talking with God. What is verbally presented to God must be taken very seriously also by the suppliant. With good reason Luther feared that where all reference to the spoken word disappears, prayer easily degenerates into a purposeless dreaming that distracts the soul instead of promoting concentration.

The prayer of supplication, especially popular in the Catholic church, took second place with Luther. But even with regard to it he strongly emphasized that its basis must be a clear conscious-

---

(*Luther,* vol. 3, p. 78), this means: "Instead (i.e., in place of the humility and contrition which he supposedly lacked), Luther formally instructs others to intersperse and enliven their prayer with curses against those of different religious views, just as he does." Is Catholicism, which makes a certain use of the anathema, really unaware that one cannot emphatically say Yes without at the same time saying No with equal emphasis? Obviously, this is all that Luther means. See *EA* 8, p. 40 (2d ed., p. 41) on his attitude toward the moral admissibility of cursing: "Thou must here distinguish between love and faith. Love must always bless, not curse. Faith has power and must curse. For faith produces children of God and stands in the place of God. Love, however, produces servants of people and stands in the place of a servant."

ness of the right to pray vouchsafed by God. Supplication has meaning and purpose only when it "proceeds from faith," that is, when it issues from full confidence that it is "pleasing to God and heard by him." Prayer from a wavering heart or petition burdened with doubt he called "adventuring" and even "tempting God."[62] While he encouraged the timid to carry everything to God with full confidence in their adoption as his children, Luther himself was well aware of what it means to present a request to the majestic God, or even to urge its timeliness. A prayer of supplication is, therefore, always a serious test of faith, and he dares to engage in it because God not only permits but even commands it. Under certain circumstances he could struggle heroically, as during his *Anfechtungen,* to pit God against God, that is, to overcome the God who seemed to be forsaking him with the God who had given his child a definite promise. But Luther also knew the purpose of this test. In contrast to Catholic custom, he insisted that what really counts is not the quantity of words nor the attempt to gain God's pity by pathetic complaints, but the powerful affect which, aware of the requirements of the case, takes repose in God's promises and finds in them the confidence of being heard. This is what Luther did in his famous prayer for Melanchthon. He felt that the issue at this moment was not simply Melanchthon's personal fate but that the great cause of the gospel was involved. There is no doubt that in this instance Luther came very close to a forcing of God. Yet we should not ignore the fact that he intended to base his prayer solely on the sure promises of God. This stipulation made it necessary for him to stop short at a certain point. When in other similar instances his prayer seemed to "bounce back," he did not become irritated but bore it with patience.[63]

---

62. For example, "The petitioner who doubts whether he is heard and prays as a kind of adventure to see if he will be heard or not is guilty on two counts. First, he nullifies his prayer. . . . Second, he treats his most faithful and true God as a liar and an unreliable person . . . and by his doubt robs God of his honor and his truthful name" (*EA* 12, p. 152; 2d ed., p. 166).
63. See *WA* 30², p. 585, ll. 11ff.: "For I think that if there were ten Moseses standing and praying for us, they would accomplish nothing. This is also how I feel when I want to pray for my dear Germany; the prayer bounces back and refuses to ascend as it does when I pray for other things." *WA,* TR 2, p. 217, l. 11: "I would very much like to see Charles prostrate

Other related questions clamored for answers when he tried to understand the world and the individual's personal fate from the standpoint of his faith in God. The goodness of God which he had felt in the depth of his heart restored to him sincere joy in the created world. He could take pleasure in every part of the creation—the silent splendor of the starry sky, the gay chatter of the birds, the majesty of the storm, all the inexhaustible wealth of nature. Yet his appreciation of nature went beyond mere observation and a purely aesthetic enjoyment. His stress on the place of the will in religious experience required this. He regarded it as a sign of growing old when he found himself innocently and without further thought taking pleasure in the flowers of his garden. Nature really became alive and meaningful for him only when he saw it as a "divine mummery." This expression brings to light another characteristic tendency in Luther's attitude toward nature, which should not be overlooked. By interpreting the world as a "mask of God" he also implied that God's majesty is revealed therein. The world does not exist only for the sake of human beings. To a certain extent the world is an end in itself. God created it in all its splendor and abundance in order to glorify himself. This outlook elevated Luther's view far above those limited considerations of the purposefulness of creation contrived by a later age, and permitted him to discover similar sentiments in the Old Testament. He prized the Psalms not only because they provide a view into every saintly soul but also because their mighty portrayals of nature elicited a deep echo in him.

Only against this background does he see the real significance of God's overflowing generosity toward human beings in creation. Thus his rejoicing in the world at once merged into his faith in providence. But here, too, it was incumbent upon him to elucidate the decisive elements. For him, faith in providence was not merely a general feeling of confidence in the course of the world, such as the Enlightenment came to affirm. Nor was it a feeling that might sporadically burst forth on particularly impressive oc-

---

the Turk; and with all my affections I pray for this. But when I pray, my prayer falls back again, for our sins are too great."

casions. In line with his interpretation of the relationship to God, Luther regarded faith in providence as a strict and ever-present duty. Just as God continues to work and to bestow gifts upon human beings out of the abundance of his goodness, so these human beings are bound to "praise and pray" at all times. Every blessing, every event in life is an opportunity to carry out the duty of recognizing and testifying that God really is God. Luther saw a remnant of original sin in the sluggish indifference of those unable to appreciate the gift and to thank the Giver for it. He severely blamed the Catholic church for its failure to place adequate stress on this most obvious practice of religion. What Luther demanded, of course, was a whole new attitude of the soul: constant attention to particular events, observation and consideration of even minute and commonplace things, a readiness to discover greatness even in the ordinary. But abilities of this kind can be developed only through serious concentration and devotion. Luther's personal practice and his ability to derive edification and a strengthening of his faith in God from everything that happened is wonderfully portrayed in the first article of his Small Catechism and in his Table Talk.

Only when the concept of evil was included, however, did this faith in providence reach its true depth. We have already shown that the actuality of evil as such gave no real offense to Luther. Yet there remained the practical question of the right inner attitude toward things that might ruin or diminish our happiness. Here, as in ethics generally, the Catholic church had followed the example of the Stoics and adopted constancy as one of the cardinal virtues. Apart from reminding the people of compensation in the life to come, Catholicism could only advise them to steel themselves and to maintain their equilibrium. Even monasticism and mysticism sought nothing more than perfect "indifference" toward all things. Luther's understanding of God led him to a much higher demand. On the one hand, he frankly recognized the experience of pain: "God does not want to tear our natural heart out of the body"; he permits us to have human feelings; he even wants us to experience pain. On the other hand, we are nevertheless honestly and joyously to affirm the ill-fortune that afflicts us, and by acknowledging God's good and gracious will even in the things that make our heart bleed, to prove our faith in God. On this point Luther was inexorable. He allowed no evasions of any kind. He himself customarily connected the adversities of the world with Satan, the hater of life. In a crass fashion reminiscent of the Greek monks, he could on occasion talk about how the devil threatens us unceasingly and overwhelms us with grief. But where the issue is one's own attitude to a personal misfortune, he rejected this approach and declared that the devil is only the tool of God; he can impose nothing on us unless God wills it. Luther went even further and stigmatized as a sinful transgression of the First Commandment any ascription of personal misfortune to the devil: the Christian in his grief is to come to terms with God and God alone. Luther also excluded the alternative favored during the Enlightenment, that the individual should take comfort in the anticipation of a restoration of his fortunes in the life to come. Now, in this very situation, God wants to be understood as gracious. Misfortune itself is to be understood as a benefit, as a blessing that furthers the recipient's development.

In the light of this demand, the cross that the Christian must bear appeared as a kind of *Anfechtung*; at least if the cross was genuine, for Luther had nothing but scorn for the self-pity that regards "every little pimple" as a cross.[64] Once again Luther saw God pitted against God—the God who, as the cause of the misfortune, appeared to be his wrathful enemy against the gracious God in whom he ought to believe. Here again it was necessary to look beyond a reality that ought not to be acknowledged as really true, to recognize God as the most gracious Father even in the cruel spectacle of his wrath, to see him in his true character "through

64. See *WA* 31¹, p. 73, l. 8: "For we are such softies and such tender martyrs; even if we have a pain in the leg or a little blister we fill heaven and earth with our cries and weepings and laments, our murmuring and our cursing, and never see how small an evil such a little blister really is, compared with the countless other goods from God which are still fully and entirely ours." The demand is even higher in *WA* 10³, p. 368, ll. 17ff.: "When I lie sick in bed, or when one is killed by fire, water, or the sword on account of his wrongdoing, this is not the cross of Christ; disgrace and persecution for righteousness' sake is the cross of Christ."

the dark glass of faith." No doubt Luther was right in saying that the fulfillment of this would be a masterpiece of faith. If trust is confidence in the good intent of another even when that person's actions seem to prove the opposite, and if the placing of such trust in another is truly to honor him, then surely life under the cross provides the opportunity to give God the highest honor. Here it would soon be revealed how much of a strain the conviction of God's goodness—received through justification—could bear. For here it was necessary to prove the purity of one's relationship to God, not only by renouncing a particular good but by giving up the whole eudaemonistic approach to life. Luther was surely right also in his further claim that the self-conquest that is a part of this faith is immeasurably greater than all the toil and self-denial of which monasticism boasted. In relation to Catholicism he found himself in a position exactly like that of Jesus as over against the Pharisees. Like Jesus, he tried to show his contemporaries that their apparently intense piety, the piety of good works, devotions, and mortifications, was actually only an evasion of the more difficult task actually required by God.[65] If Luther was deeply offended by the Catholic pose of public or secret pride in "heroic" achievements, this also corresponded fully to the spirit of Jesus.

But if Luther was right in his vigorous reinterpretation of the moral demands implicit in faith in God and in his effort to show how they constantly confront us in our everyday existence, then every event, every encounter with God, leads us back again to our own inwardness. This is especially true of a personal cross. Only when we recognize such discipline as salutary can we honestly affirm our cross and regard what is repugnant to us as grace. Luther viewed this soul-searching induced by the "sacrament of the cross," as he was inclined to call it, as an essential part of the intended blessing. He did not believe that every adversity was a punishment for a specific sin that the person should search out and identify, although such a thing could happen. In such an instance Luther required the believer willingly to accept the punishment

---

65. The whole of Luther's *Treatise on Good Works* develops this idea.

laid upon him by God and not to try to alleviate it, as the Catholic offer of indulgences seemed to suggest. However, he emphasized a more profound general principle. Our affectations disappear as we are compelled to bear the cross, as we encounter what we would rather avoid. Then we see ourselves as we really are. By looking at our own spontaneous behavior, our rising passion, the temptation to hate God, and the difficulty with which we submit to God, we can discern which will is actually dominant in us, the one that says yes to God or the one oriented to the self. The cross, however, brings only those things to light which every observant person might perceive in his own practice of the faith, indeed in his every prayer. For who has really attained constant trust in God, full inner freedom and joy, and the perfect will to serve God as he should be served? Who could help noticing how much in us is dead, half-hearted, selfish? When the conscience is sharpened through contact with God in prayer—and who can stand before God without experiencing this?—we find that even after we have done a good deed we somehow feel that we owe God something more. Even the believer still sins in every good work.[66] The very best that we do is still infected with an egotism that ought to be conquered. Anyone who could glory in feeling the impulses of the Holy Spirit should experience this most strongly.[67]

Someone less courageous might well have concluded that the whole struggle is in vain and that one must resign oneself to one's limitations, including those of one's moral resources. But neither Luther's faith nor his conscience would permit such resignation. The task remained unchanged even though it seemed impossible of fulfillment, for what is impossible with human beings is possible with God. From the fact that the "old being" continually reappears even in the believer, Luther only inferred the necessity of continually returning to the beginning, namely, to the reestablish-

---

66. Denifle (*Luther und Lutherthum,* 2d ed., vol. 1, pp. 503ff.) treats this statement as if it were a kind of blasphemy.

67. See *WA* 12, p. 573, l. 26: "There must always be such a mixture that we feel both, the Holy Spirit and our sin and imperfection. For it must be with us as it is with someone sick who is in the hands of the physician but is expected to get better."

ment of one's relationship to God. For Luther, "justification" was not something that works itself out automatically once it has been experienced. It was rather an ever-recurring event that receives its special meaning and increasing profundity from the particular impressions of the respective moment. Paradoxical as it may at first seem, Luther saw in these continual "new starts" the indispensable method for genuine inner progress. If the defect is in the person, the ego, then true ethical advance can take place only if this ego itself is constantly renewed. It is not enough that particular aspects of a person are improved, much less that the sum total of good works is increased, as the Catholic church imagined. The ultimate motives must be reached, which dominate us even without our being aware of them. Justification, if a person takes it seriously, means a going back to one's innermost being in the sight of God; the whole person emerges renewed; the selfless ego that is entirely devoted to God is born ever anew, and from the deepened relationship to God it derives the power to conquer the natural, selfish ego.

Because of the tension created by a goal that is always fully obligatory and yet never really attained, piety became for Luther the highest kind of inner vitality, a restless movement. "Being a Christian is not a matter of being, but rather of becoming" is an ever-recurring refrain in Luther's writings. There is no standing still at any stage of accomplishment. Even what seems to be purest must be transcended. "To have God" necessarily leads to renewed search for him. The self-awareness of the believer, therefore, is always twofold in character, namely, simultaneously as saint and sinner. And the believer really is both at the same time: still the self-seeking ego, and yet also the one whom God has accepted, who is being sanctified through fellowship with him. The more clearly one sees these two aspects in one, that is, the more honestly one faces one's own guilt and the mercy by which one is sustained, the more healthy is one's inner life. But reliance upon the power of fellowship with God must be the stronger element. In spite of all disappointments and defeats, the sense of victory, even over the power of sin, ought to be maintained in the believer, or else continually restored. Luther saw the ultimate proof of it in the believer's finding the courage to look forward to death, since it brings him release from original sin.

7. Luther's Concept of Christian Activity

Seen from this vantage point, religion is simply passivity,[68] complete inwardness, unconditional trust in the goodness of God even when his actions are initially unintelligible, humble patience toward the God who in judgment and mercy uses the fortunes of life and the power of conscience to change our refractory earthly nature into the image of his own. Luther strongly emphasized this passive side of religion. It remained all-important for him, the very breath of religion. Yet his faith in God also contained the strongest impulses toward fruitful expression of the inward experience in active work for God.[69] But what is meant by working for God? How does the duty to act acquire a specific content? When is a possible course of action a real service to God? Luther had to embark on a detailed analysis of the whole accepted order of life and society before he could give the simple answer implied by his basic principles. Here, too, we see him proceeding steadily, taking the heart of the matter as his point of departure.

Luther's experience of God, in contrast to what seemed natural to the mystics, was never of a kind to permit him to think of God as his own exclusive possession. He was convinced that what he had found could and should be found by everyone. God's gifts of forgiveness and community with himself were vouchsafed not only

68. Of course, there are different kinds of passivity. Luther's is not dull or indolent but is extremely active.
69. It is customary to use Calvin as the standard for measuring Luther, and then to characterize Lutheran piety as resigned and Calvinist piety as activist. But this is to misread the historical relationship. In order properly to appreciate Luther he must be seen against the background of Catholic piety and especially mysticism. Against this background, it is immediately apparent that it was Luther who first introduced the notion of activism into religion. Calvin only went further in the way pioneered by Luther.

to him but to all. For spiritual blessings are essentially communal blessings. It is part of their character that they bind together those who share them, and that they grow only as many come to participate in them, since no one person can exhaust their depth. Although it is correct to say that every believer has Christ wholly, it is equally true that no one has Christ wholly. The individual's comprehension is always one-sided and needs to be supplemented by what others have received. Furthermore, God indeed follows a unique course with every person and assigns each one a special task, but what the individual has received attains its full worth only when it benefits others. Everyone, therefore, must use the gift to help others. Especially the "strong" ought to feel responsible to support the "weak." Anyone who wants to live a solitary life is guilty of intolerable arrogance that endangers the soul.[70]

The community concept is thus an essential part of Luther's piety, and a part which he underscored heavily. Always an opponent of selfishness, Luther was especially opposed to the religious selfishness whose only concern is one's own salvation. A true Christian seeks the salvation of others as much as one's own; according to Romans 9:3, one should even be ready to sacrifice one's own salvation if others could thereby be saved. Nothing could be further from the truth than to see only the individualist in Luther. One is inclined to say, on the contrary, that precisely because he was so pronounced an individualist who based everything on the personal conscience, he was also the principal advocate of the community concept in religion. No one saw more clearly than he the weaknesses and dangers of an exclusive individualism. It was he and none other who overcame the individualism of the mystics and of the Renaissance.

These convictions received more definite form as Luther came to grips with the prevailing concept of the church. In the visible church as such he failed to recognize that inner union of souls which his community concept envisaged. The visible Catholic

---

70. Already in the Lectures on the Psalms, Luther attacked the *singulares,* or *monii*—this could be translated "individualists"—in a similar spirit. See *WA, TR* 2, p. 462, ll. 7ff.: ". . . and Christ's life was wholly social." . . .

church was a legal entity in which the personal relationship of the individual to Christ and the faith was in principle immaterial. But for Luther this was the main thing: only a community whose members were actually united with God deserved to be called a church of Christ. Only such members were ruled by Christ, and only they were able to engage in the spiritual intercourse that was so important to Luther.

This concern led Luther not to the idea of a sect made up only of the elect but to the reassertion of Augustine's distinction between the visible and the invisible church. The totality of those who have been inwardly laid hold of by God is the true church, even though it is invisible. It is the kingdom of God, to use a biblical expression Luther liked. In comparison with it, the visible church is only a copy, a more or less useful instrument. Yet Luther invests the idea of the invisible church with all the ethical content furnished him by his understanding of the gospel. Augustine had already referred to the spirit of love which permeates the members of the true church and unites their hearts. As usual, Luther is more definite. For here, too, his restoration of the New Testament concept of love in all its absoluteness is relevant. To him, the members of the invisible church are those who, conscious of their common destiny and of the undeserved grace they have received, regard other human beings as their brothers and sisters, and community with them as far more important than personal gain. They devote everything they have, therefore, from external goods to the most deeply spiritual treasures, to the service of the neighbor; and they are able to sacrifice every right, honor, and possession in order to overcome by kindness those who are of a hostile disposition.

Thought out along these lines, the idea of the invisible church became the center of all of Luther's thinking about the world that surrounded him. He did not hesitate to employ the traditional claim of the church that it represented the very purpose for which God created the world and the human race. Even though the invisible church might seem to some to reflect too modest an understanding of the church, Luther felt that if absolute value can be predicated of anything existing in this world, it is of this highest form of divine-human community. However, his insistence that God himself was the Creator of the invisible church implied two further conclusions. First, the church is not merely an idea or an ultimate goal; it is a present reality. In fact, it has to be real, if God is the Almighty One. The irresistible power of the divine word which Luther had experienced surely was also operative for others. Wherever God sent forth his word—and the gospel had already been working powerfully for centuries—there would have to be people who were influenced and led to God by it. This view was also supported by Luther's personal experience. In every kind word spoken to him by another, in every sincere service rendered him by someone else, in every intercessory prayer of a friend through which he was strengthened, in every worship service that conveyed the experience of soul being joined to soul, he perceived that community in God was a present reality and that among his acquaintances were some who belonged to the kingdom of God and in whom God's Spirit was active. Secondly, it was also true that God's kingdom was not yet complete; neither externally—for the gospel had by no means permeated the entire world—nor internally. Just as the individual continued to stand in need of cleansing even though he was a "saint," so did the whole community also. The invisible church—note well, the invisible, not the visible church—was a hospital in which Christ as the Good Samaritan bestowed care and healing.

Reference to this work of Christ gave concrete precision to Luther's concept of God as the living God who is unceasingly active. Now Luther saw God's activity not only behind the mask of the external creation but also within human hearts. The latter activity was not, of course, discernible by the senses, as was the former. Only faith could detect that activity. Yet that was the activity that God carried on as his very own. And there were plenty of signs of both his wrath and his grace in human affairs. It was at this point that Luther found the motive for human activity.

Now the notion of the divine monergism, which Luther had again employed so meaningfully in his concept of the invisible church, might have led to quietism. It did, in fact, have this effect in the later Orthodoxy and in Pietism, even in Reformed Pietism. It is characteristic of Luther, however, that he, like Paul, drew the opposite conclusion. The idea of God's monergism was too closely connected in his mind with his sense of human responsibility. God indeed worked all in all, but in regard to human beings—at least in the case of the elect—he worked by awakening the conscience. The fact that God brought human beings into relation with himself also implied that he intended to make use of them: they were to be not only vessels but also instruments. This is why God granted them his gifts and the free delight to do his will, in order that they might do their part. If God did not rest, they dared not be idle. The believer was under the same obligation to increase the inheritance as the child in the home.

This understanding transformed the sense of a vital community with God and elation over the grace received into a delight in work. The building of the invisible church was the divine work in which every Christian was called to take part. Any inner or outer distress on the part of another human being, any fault in the religious or moral life, now imposed a responsibility. Whoever noticed such needs had the duty to do his part to meet them. Here was an opportunity for the employment of every possible gift. Luther used the strongest possible expressions to stress the gloriousness of this kind of service. Everyone may be a Christ to others; occasionally Luther, not without biblical warrant, even ventures the bold assertion that one may become "God" for another. A person may manifest greatness by exercising, like God, patience and forgiveness; gifts out of God's treasure-house may be dispensed; even life may be created and called forth, as by God himself.[71]

71. Luther's biblical authorities for this expression are Psalm 82:6 (as with the Greek monks) and Exodus 4:16 and 7:1. As for the meaning, see WA 4, p. 280, ll. 2f.: "In the same way every Christian ought to acknowledge himself to be great, because, on account of the faith of Christ dwelling in him, he is God, son of God, and infinite, because God is now in him. Therefore everyone of his persecutors is to him like a bee, whom he ought to receive magnanimously, without thinking much of him, asking deliverance from him in the name of the Lord. For this word consoles us and exhorts us unto patience." WA 11¹, p. 100, ll. 18ff.: "We are gods through love, which makes us beneficent toward our neighbor; for the divine

Thus Luther provided a basis for the duty to act, a duty—and I should like to emphasize this—which Luther always regarded as primary. The resulting kind of activity, however, was limited to the spiritual realm, to the inner advancement of other human beings. It remained an open question, or rather it now became a crucial one, how ordinary secular work was related to this activity in the kingdom of God. Did it imply a withdrawal from God or at least a declension that ought to be avoided as much as possible?

It was not hard for Luther to attain clarity on the general issues involved. It was evident that even the spiritual kingdom could not exist unless there were people and unless they were supported by work. Luther was also able to oppose successfully the objection that worldly activity in itself leads one away from God. His concept of faith broke through the wall that the Catholic church had erected between sacred and secular activity. If faith was the most important thing to God and the best way of honoring him, then the kind of work one did—great or small, sacred or secular—was no longer the important consideration. Lowly service could be spiritual activity in the highest sense if it was done to fulfill one's God-given duty. Moreover, only by taking the cares and burdens of the world upon oneself would one experience the tests of faith which could prove whether one's trust in God was really pure and complete. So Luther came to the valid conclusion that activity in the world leads one closer to God than monastic escape from the world. In contrast to monasticism's preferred status in the Catholic church, ordinary work in society was elevated to the level of a "vocation" in the full sense of the word—a commission, a mandate from God to the individual which must not be evaded.

Yet a person's specific vocation was not assigned directly by God. Specific vocation was mediated through the political and social order, which thereby asserted its sovereign claim and the

---

nature is nothing other than pure beneficence." The expression affords us a perspective on Luther's position in the history of religion. If one recalls how deification has been interpreted in the history of Christianity—as "becoming immortal" or "being filled with mysterious, supernatural powers," in the Catholic church; as "conquering the passions and thus also nature," in monasticism; as "becoming one with the infinite," in mysticism—then it becomes clear how far Luther's concept of deification, "becoming a benefactor for others," surpasses all that had come before.

resulting activity in turn became a part of this comprehensive order. Was it possible and necessary for someone like Luther, who affirmed the world as God's creation and activity in the world as service to God, also to approve the whole humanly instituted order of society just as he found it? Now Luther confronted the really difficult questions. He had already caused a deep rift in the prevailing order by depriving the visible church of its standing as a divine institution. Could the rest remain as it was? To believe that once Luther had dethroned the church everything else fell into place is to miss part of Luther's greatest accomplishment. The difficult questions with which the ancient church had wrestled now confronted him in all their starkness. His new understanding of the claims of the gospel made it possible for him to see the disparity between the Christian way of life and worldly society in more profound terms than any of his predecessors, including Augustine. If the kingdom of God is a covenanted community where everything is based on the voluntary principle and every sacrifice ought to be made cheerfully for the neighbor, how can it be harmonized with the state whose citizens—including the Christians!—are held together by coercion and force? What about the law that supports one person's self-assertion as over against another's? Above all, what about war? What about economic life, which flourishes when private profit is pursued as the immediate goal? Can there be two orders in the world? Is not the order of the kingdom of God the only one that God approves and therefore the only legitimate one? The Anabaptists were not the first to raise these questions. Luther pondered them long before they did. In fact, without Luther, who taught them how to interpret the gospel and the Sermon on the Mount, neither they nor their successors (including Tolstoy) would ever have arrived at their ideas.

Luther himself never succumbed to the temptation of wanting to replace the legal and economic orders with the gospel. He rejected this idea even when it was directly urged upon him during the Peasants' War and even though by this rejection he risked all his previous popularity. But he stood fast—for the sake of the gospel itself. It was quite clear to him that the gospel is concerned not simply with certain acts but with the motives behind them. The gospel's requirements are met only when they are fulfilled with full inner freedom, out of the pure enthusiasm of the heart. He saw that this all-important feature would be threatened if the gospel became a social order, a law to which all would have to submit whether they wanted to or not. This would inevitably turn the gospel into a form of compulsion, a "law," which was bound (according to Luther) to produce only hypocrites. At the very least, both piety and morals would be in danger of degenerating into legalism.

Nor was it any more tolerable to regard the gospel and the forms of life in the world as unrelated entities, for this could either force Christians back into renunciation of the world or, if they were advised to accommodate themselves to both, result in a divided life and a divided conscience. Luther found the answer by starting with the undeniable fact that, numerically, the kingdom of God always lags behind humanity as a whole. The whole world will never really be won for the gospel in the sense of a deep inner acceptance of its teaching. There will always be non-Christians, even within so-called Christendom. In fact, even where the gospel is externally in control, the non-Christians will actually constitute the majority. Thus Luther interpreted the New Testament statement about the few who are chosen, and found confirmation in the fact that a significant number of people lack the most basic requirement, a living personal conscience. This painful observation was the main stimulus for Luther's belief in a secret decree of God.

He had to regard it as a disastrous self-deception, therefore, to base the regulation of natural human social life even within "Christendom" on the assumption that all its members are really Christians, people who voluntarily do their duty to their neighbor even at a personal sacrifice. A sober estimate of things would rather have to assume that the majority always obeys its selfish motives and never voluntarily rises above the maintenance of a certain external propriety.

This is why, according to Luther, government and law are necessary. Both are indispensable in order peacefully to unite people who otherwise would mangle and grind one another, and to establish a basis for material progress. Force and coercion must be employed because some people understand no other language. Patiently to wait for such people to be converted and healed of their wild impulses through internally operative forces would be to share the responsibility for all the crimes they would commit in the meantime. For these reasons Luther also asserted unambiguously that government and law function on a lower level than gospel and church. To be sure, insofar as the state is conducive to human well-being, it is ordained of God. But the state is not a divine order of the highest rank; it is not a part of God's "proper" will. Luther did not hesitate to apply the distinction between the "proper work" and the "alien work," between wrath and grace, which had been so important for his concept of God, to the relationship between the state and the kingdom of God. The state belongs to the lower level. Through it, that is, through its penal power, the wrath of God is poured out over a sinful humanity.

Just as he had seen more than the destructive aspect of God's wrath, however, so Luther also saw an aspect of government and law which connects them with the gospel and helps to promote it. The peace that the state promotes is one of the conditions for the growth, and even for the survival, of the kingdom of God on earth. Without the intervention of the state, Christians, who themselves are not allowed to resist injustice, would be wholly without protection against being exploited by the violent. As individuals they could bear such exposure. But since selfish people constitute the majority, the overall result would be the extermination of Christians. That would also mean the end of the gospel. Since the state averts all this and ensures peace in the world, it becomes God's instrument for preserving the gospel. Moreover, the state itself brings a part of God's love to realization. The protection it gives to the weak, the care it exercises for the physical welfare of its subjects, the sense of community it fosters, are proofs of goodness and humanitarian concern even though they deal only with externals.

Luther courageously spelled out the implications for the behavior of Christians. He was not willing to urge upon them the hypocritical role of benefiting from the existence of the state while leaving its unpleasant tasks to others. If the activity of the state benefits Christianity, then true Christians not only may but must participate in it—whether as officials, judges, soldiers, or even hangmen. Christians may assume such positions in good conscience and must invest in them all the devotion and fidelity to which their religion commits them. By doing so, they serve God and, even though individual cases may seem to prove otherwise, they exercise love toward their neighbors at the same time. One must not think of a criminal being punished only as an individual. A Christian judge ought not, of course, to ignore the effect of harsh treatment on the criminal's soul. But if the whole of society is kept in mind, for whose sake severe measures are sometimes necessary, it becomes plain that society's preservation is tantamount to protection of the neighbor and to that extent is true love.

Thus Luther pointed out the plain objectives of God-directed action. He firmly related direct activity for the kingdom of God, through spiritual influence on other human beings, with social and vocational endeavors. Yet Luther stressed two further conditions that determine whether activity in a secular calling is really service to God.

First: Luther's affirmation, described above, of the secular orders as divine orders meant neither that the individual as a private citizen could always make use of all his legal rights nor that the bearers of public office could in their official capacity regard regulations in force at a given moment as immutable natural law. Luther justified the state, the law, and economic activity by indicating how each served the objectives of love. In doing so, he also meant to set up a standard of judgment. The individual must deliberate which approach—insistence on one's rights or renunciation of them—will best serve the purposes of love, that is, the inner advancement of one's neighbor, at a given moment. The government must engage in similar deliberation. It is likewise bound to proceed in the direction of love and therefore to eliminate inhuman, cruel, and irrational elements in existing law. Luther himself made a number of specific proposals along this line. He, the conservative, thereby became the advocate of progress.[72]

The second point is even more important. His demonstration of the importance of the state, the law, and the economy showed only that secular work *can be* service to God, not that it always *is*. Even the most faithful performance of vocational duties and the most conscientious fulfillment of one's obligations to the prince can still be firmly rooted in selfishness. Religion, or service to God, is only that activity which is consciously related to God and which seeks only his glory.[73] Luther never tired of emphasizing the importance of this point. At stake here was the high point of his conception of faith, and yet he felt that he was merely trying to establish a truth so self-evident that only a dullard could be unmindful of it. The Scholastics had seemed to say the same thing. They, too, taught that everything must be done to the glory of God. But they regarded an occasional act of conscious love to God as satisfying the requirements of duty in the strict sense, while the rest of the time the residual attitude, the so-called "virtual" or "habitual" good intention, sufficed to establish the necessary reference of an act to God. Once again Luther required everything. In one's activity, just as in one's passivity, everything ultimately depends upon the conscious personal relationship with God. He was fortified by Paul's statement in Romans 14:23 that an act which does not proceed from faith is actually sin. Yet he did more than simply draw from this passage the general thought that it is an essential duty somehow to refer every act to God. He

72. One of Troeltsch's greatest weaknesses in his *Social Teaching of the Christian Churches* (London: Allen & Unwin, 1931) is his almost complete neglect of this side of Luther. He always lumps Luther together with Melanchthon and Orthodoxy, reading their ideas back into him. But this destroys Luther's unique greatness; nowhere are those areas in which Luther towers above his successors given their due. Troeltsch's fear of modernizing Luther, which stands behind his approach, is commendable and fine. But it must not lead us to represent Luther as more medieval than he really was.
73. It is one of the peculiar biases of contemporary scholarship to look upon the formula "seeking the glory of God" as a "Calvinistic" concept. Did not 1 Corinthians 10:31 and Colossians 3:17—where the concept originates—play a role throughout the Scholastic period? My essay on "Der Neubau der Sittlichkeit" [The reconstruction of morality] in *GA* 1, pp. 155ff., will trace Luther's critique of the Scholastic treatment of the concept and show in what sense Luther accepted it. Here, too, Calvin only continued Luther's work.

found in it the more profound idea that every deed must be sustained by the conviction that this very act is "acceptable and pleasing to God." Luther meant that the believer must be the conscious executor of God's will. Only then does activity become a divine service in the true sense.

Concentration on this requirement turns every effort to relate an act to God into a probing of the conscience. It breaks through the heedlessness that accepts a goal from habit or natural instinct and compels a person continually to reassert the principle of action at its highest level—from the viewpoint of God's will and the personal relationship to God—even with regard to commonplace things. It was axiomatic for Luther that the simple, homely duties implicit in the ordinary relationships of life take precedence over sensational deeds. God's will is most likely to be found in simple things. When these simple tasks are consciously affirmed as God's will, their performance, even when required by one's calling, is accompanied by the feeling of freedom; and there is always strength enough to extend concern for the neighbor even beyond the bounds of one's vocation. Where circumstances require it, this feeling of freedom can inspire one's courage to the point of taking on even unusual tasks—tasks that fly in the face of tradition—in the name of one's vocation. For if God is alive and working, always opening up new possibilities and making new things necessary, and if the believer may act consciously as an instrument of God, then there may be instances where duty will be perceived to require actions that, according to the standard of the "law," are wrong. But woe to whoever presumes to do this with wicked intent!

Thus Luther's consideration of secular activity again returned to the personal level, to the inner self, to the living conscience. As he described the royal freedom of action, Luther retracted none of his earlier statements about the insufficiency of all human works and the necessity of constant repentance. He did not see contradiction here but harmony. Freedom and self-assurance, although gifts of God, were for him things that always needed to be acquired through constant self-improvement. The more one is liberated from the self through repentance, and the more hum-

107

bly one bows before God and is renewed by him, the more quickly will God's will be discerned in particular situations and the freedom to affirm it be attained. Luther's ideal was a state of mind in which one's entire consciousness is pervaded by spontaneity, where the right is discerned without lengthy deliberation. "Faith does not ask whether good works ought to be done but does them before there is time to ask; faith is always found in action." In this state of mind, there is a coincidence of opposites: conscious of being but the mask of God, one is nevertheless most truly oneself; one's activity is wholly passive, and one's passivity wholly active.

Now, with this understanding of religion, what was Luther's attitude to the progressive spirit of his day? He was able to go along with it for quite a distance. The attitude he had attained toward secular activity led him not only to hail the upsurge of culture but even to provide it with strong new stimuli all along the line. In the manner of Hutten he could speak of the golden age in which his generation lived, and in spite of his ridicule of Copernicus he included the advance of the natural sciences in this judgment. There was no area of culture that was not fertilized by his ideas.[74] Conversely, whatever in his day sought freedom and personal self-development found religious support in the movement he had inaugurated.

Yet at the most profound level he found himself in conscious and express opposition to the current of his time. It is the grossest misunderstanding of Luther to make him and his work the product of the so-called "general feeling for life" of his day. The truth is that he opposed this feeling with all his might. He did not merely consummate something already present in his time; he brought to the fore something distinctive and much more important. He himself was under the impression, which Nietzsche later confirmed in his own way, that without him his age would have succumbed to epicureanism. His deep awareness of the danger of reaching the point of cultural satiety was not the only reason for

74. See my essay "Die Kulturbedeutung der Reformation" (*The Cultural Significance of the Reformation* [New York: Meridian Books, 1959]) in *GA* 1, pp. 468–543.

this judgment. He also felt, with good cause, that at the very point where he and the advancing culture seemed to come together they were actually far apart.

It was not by accident that he came into conflict with Erasmus, the noblest representative of religious humanism, and that he carried on this controversy with unusual earnestness and religious power. In Erasmus Luther attacked "enlightened" religion, not because he himself was too medieval to appreciate it, but because he had a more profound understanding of the essence of religion. The Renaissance wanted to make religion a part of culture. It wanted to develop traditional Christianity by obliterating its distinctive elements in favor of a common religion of humanity. Luther moved in the opposite direction. With primitive Christianity as his source, he reaffirmed the powerful motives that distinguish Christianity from all other religions and allowed them full sway. Relentlessly he emphasized that the concern of religion is not whether I want to have anything to do with God but whether God wants to have anything to do with me, the individual human being. Religion thus takes the form of a struggle— a life-and-death struggle—between a person and God. It demands, even when peace with God has been attained, the commitment of the total personality. For the faith in which religion culminates is always a conquest of powers that are operative in and around us, which we can only master by permitting ourselves to be completely overcome by God. But this characteristic sets religion apart from every other human concern and makes it unique. Religion can never be merely an aspect of civilization, a mere "cultural religion" [*Bildungsreligion*]. Religion is either ultimate personal concern or it has no meaning at all. When it is only one concern among others it loses its seriousness and finally degenerates into a feeble type of self-enjoyment. This is the message that made Luther the great awakener of the conscience in his day. It brings him as close to our generation as to his own.[75]

75. The question of Luther's relation to the Middle Ages has been raised again by Ernst Troeltsch. But the discussions of recent years seem to have demonstrated that a "scientific" solution of this problem is wholly impos-

One important question remains. Is this interpretation of religion distinctively German to the degree that it can be really meaningful only to a German? The courage to bear personal responsibility, the determination to think things through completely, the ability to embrace contradictories in one single vision, equal appreciation for the heroic and the tender, and the emotional ardor that permeates all—these are most assuredly German. So also are the inclination to melancholy, the propensity for brooding which is stirred into action only by the strongest pressure of the conscience, the angularity of his ideas, and the violence of his utterance. Nevertheless, we would be arrogant and at the same time betray a lack of appreciation for Luther's greatness if we Germans laid claim to him for ourselves alone. It becomes very evident in him how that which issues from the profound genius of a people also has within it the universally human element. Even in the early years of his career, Luther's ideas penetrated far beyond German lands, to the Low Countries, France, England, Scandinavia, Italy, and even to Spain, arousing people's hearts and laying hold of them. This simple fact proves that Luther's interpretation of religion, even though it issued from the depths of his own heart, has universal human appeal. Luther belongs not only to us Germans, he belongs to humanity. This is why we are confident that his attainments will continue to be cherished.

---

sible, since the scholar's own attitude to ultimate questions inevitably colors his conclusions. . . . If the essential Christian dualism and its presupposition, the absolutely valid moral law and an understanding of sin based on this absolutely valid moral law, have been decisively refuted by the intellectual developments beginning with the Enlightenment—and this is evidently not the view of Troeltsch himself—then Luther indeed does belong to the Middle Ages. The Reformation would then be regarded as the last convulsive attempt of Christianity to maintain itself against the demands for the autonomy of human life. If, on the other hand, Christianity is regarded as unconquered and its concepts as normative, then Luther stands out so sharply from the Middle Ages and appears so much as the transformer of the whole life of the mind that it is impossible to associate him with the Middle Ages. His conceiving of religion primarily in terms of conscience signifies—despite his biblicism . . .—the decisive breakthrough, not only with respect to the Middle Ages, but with respect to the whole standpoint of the Catholic church; it provides at the same time the foundation for an autonomy that is more than merely an imperfect preliminary form of the autonomy espoused by the Enlightenment.

Appendix

Gogarten's Understanding of Luther

Friedrich Gogarten has commented on my volume of Luther studies from his own peculiar theological standpoint.[1] I do not mind replying to him, for in so doing I have the opportunity to make even clearer the points at which we differ. Gogarten thinks that the fundamental fault of my understanding of Luther consists in my asserting that "Luther's faith is essentially moral in character," or in other words, that I am "deriving Luther's views from a fundamental moral experience." My doing so is said to show "the dominant influence of the Kantian doctrine of the primacy of the moral"; but as a result of this influence I am said to have misunderstood the significance of the gospel for Luther and for theology generally.

Before I enter into the substance of the discussion, it seems necessary—in view also of Hermelink's review of my book[2]—to clarify first of all how the term "moral" is being used. Those who remember the controversy about Ritschl's theology will recall that this term was being used by both sides in such a way that they often talked past each other, because they attached different meanings to the term. Now Gogarten, appealing to Heinrich Barth, states that "the fundamental principle of the science of ethics"—that is, Kant's categorical imperative—signifies "the negation of the present material reality of life," a demand, an "ought," and thus a negation of the given and a position only in the sense of the affirmation of a not-given. By way of contrast, the gospel is said to speak "of that which science knows only as not-given, as demand, as judgment, as sublation, as negation, precisely as affirmation, as fulfillment, as grace, as gift, as given."

This definition of the "moral" strikes me as very general indeed. In any case, it does not by any means express what is distinctive in Kant's

---

1. EDITORS' NOTE: Gogarten's critique of the first volume of Holl's collected essays appeared under the title "Theologie und Wissenschaft: Grundsätzliche Bemerkungen zu Karl Holls 'Luther,' " in *Die Christliche Welt* 38 (1924): cols. 34–42, 71–80.

2. EDITORS' NOTE: Heinrich Hermelink's critique appeared as "Ein Wendepunkt in der Lutherforschung" in *Die Christliche Welt* 38 (1924): cols. 99–108.

ethic, if I understand Kant correctly. Ethical systems differ both in the way in which they determine the *rule* of action—whether it be happiness, inner harmony, or whatever—and the *motivation* for action which they require or presuppose as present in us in order that we may accept this rule. If it is true that morality always aims at a formation of the will, and moreover, that the ultimately determinative factor is the motivation, then the second element is even more important than the first. Kant's undeniable historical merit is to have again defined submission to something unconditional as the true meaning of morality. But Kant indicates that the reason we submit to that unconditional something is our regard for our own "dignity," that is, our self-respect. Because of this latter element I have always unmistakably rejected Kantian ethics. Anyone who has read even my essay "The Reconstruction of Morality" [*Der Neubau der Sittlichkeit*] will confirm this. For self-respect derives from self-love, and such a morality is nothing other than a refined self-love, as Kant himself is at one point forced to admit. When I rejected Kant, moreover, I thereby rejected every philosophical ethic.[3] For no philosophical ethic—that is, none that takes human nature as its point of departure—can possibly discover a higher motivation than self-respect. The type of ethic popular today, which prefers to speak of "values" rather than of a moral law, brings this out even more clearly than does the Kantian ethic. For when I recognize "values" I am at the same time trying to increase my own value.

Christianity recognizes a higher concept of the moral. Its morality lies from the outset on a different level, because its point of departure is God, or, more precisely, God's gift. Life itself and all that belongs to it are viewed as God's gift—compare Luther's exposition of the First Article [of the Creed, in his Small Catechism]—but above and beyond these the really decisive gift is the gospel, that is, the community with God resulting from the forgiveness of sins. Yet the gift immediately gives rise to a demand, to an "ought," but not, however, in the Enlightenment sense of an obligation henceforth to lead a "moral," virtuous life. What is implied is something much simpler and closer at hand, namely, the duty to recognize in the gift God as the Giver and to honor him accordingly. This is his purpose in giving his gift—in order that we may find God. God wants to be recognized by us and to be honored by us through gratitude. For only this understanding on our part and our appropriate response bring about what God's gift ultimately aims at: personal community between ourselves and God. Where this duty is not perceived, God's gift is deprived of

---

3. See *GA* 1, pp. 155–287. Gogarten and I also differ in the way we use the term "science" (*Wissenschaft*). For Gogarten, "science" also includes ethics. I regard it as constitutive for science that it is able to *compel* assent to its conclusions. This is not true of ethics. Ethical assertions always depend for their recognition on the other person's *will*. This is why I do not speak of "scientific" but rather of philosophical ethics.

its meaning and its seriousness. Now insofar as the conscience[4] represents our receptivity toward the "ought," I have called Luther's religion, which gives the strongest possible emphasis to this feature, a religion of conscience. But by doing so I did not think myself guilty of "trespassing into another area" [as Gogarten had charged], but rather thought I was working out precisely what makes Luther's religion a religion, a relationship to God. The motivation for this "ought" is clearly differentiated from the motivation of philosophical ethics. For here people are motivated not by self-respect but by gratitude, which implies that if there is genuine obedience toward the "ought," it is also spontaneous and joyful and devoid of all self-interest.

I had indicated that there is no continuity between these two forms of morality, the philosophical and the Christian. One gets from one to the other only by a break—by a break with self-love. For in one case the relationship to oneself is what is decisive; in the other, the relationship to God. Consequently the two views necessarily condemn each other. Philosophical ethics strikes the Christian ethicist as irreligious, for if it is the aim of a philosophical ethic to facilitate the increase of one's own value, then precisely at the point where it would seem to become religious it actually becomes irreligious, yielding to the tempter's promise, "Ye shall be as gods. . . ." Self-glorification takes the place of the awareness that all one is and has is a gift, or grace. Conversely, the philosopher will always be inclined to regard Christian ethics as inferior, as "heteronomous"; whether he is justified in doing so is another question.

Now there is room for argumentation as to whether or not it is appropriate to use the term "moral" for what I have called the morality of Christianity. For the "ought" that makes its appearance in Christianity differs in all decisive points from what is elsewhere understood by "moral" and "morality." In Christianity, even the will that recognizes duty and affirms it is regarded as produced by God himself, through his gift. In order to avoid misunderstanding as much as possible, I have therefore refrained as much as I could from using the term "moral," and have preferred to speak generally of duty and the "ought."[5] Still, insofar as the gospel addresses itself to the will

---

4. Gogarten always thinks of the conscience in terms of the accusing conscience. He nowhere takes note of the fact that conscience can also be understood differently, namely, as the feeling of responsibility, the sense of obligation.

5. This is also why I cannot agree with Hermelink when he designates my understanding of Luther "as the culmination, in a way, of the process of ethicizing Luther that had been begun by Ritschl"; I am said to have presented Luther as the restorer of "the perfect ethical religion of Jesus." This is not the place to discuss Ritschl and his understanding of Luther. I, for my part, do not see Luther's Reformation principle in his restoration of an ethical religion—insofar as the "ethical" and "morality" are understood as something separate from religion which nevertheless ennobles religion by being incorporated in it—but rather in this, that he gave a more profound

and presents to it a goal—namely, God and community with him—which must be affirmed by us, the term "moral" may be used in this connection. What I could not have been prepared for, however, is that I should be accused of understanding Luther's ethic "as a refinement of natural morality into Christian morality."[6]

The deficiency of my understanding of Luther becomes particularly evident, according to Gogarten, where I try to understand the process of justification. In order to illuminate this process, I had stressed as particularly important those passages in which Luther describes the highest stage of his *Anfechtungen*; namely, those moments when Christ himself recedes from his view and he confronts God directly and alone. In such instances, according to Luther's own statement, his ultimate refuge is the First Commandment, or, more precisely, its opening words: "I am the Lord, thy God." This commandment has a liberating effect on Luther insofar as the obligation to comply with it never ceases at any time or for any person. According to Luther, this implies that the stance adopted by God toward him ("I am the Lord, *thy* God") continues to prevail, even in regard to himself, even in this moment of affliction: God calls him through this commandment into his service; thus God wants to let him live in his sight. This would actually signify the forgiveness of sins.

I had expressly warned that this process should not be regarded as a "rational inference from the fact of the moral consciousness," even though it appears in the form of an inference. For what is involved, according to Luther's own words, is something that is not only against all reason but also against his own conscience, indeed against God himself. Luther is to "believe" that God is gracious toward him even though his conscience testifies clearly and distinctly—and as he is forced to admit, rightly—that he stands under God's wrath.

Now Gogarten finds that what I am describing is nevertheless nothing other than a "rational inference from the fact of the moral consciousness." He even claims that I in effect admit this when I say: "This (namely, that God, as he testifies through his commandment, is maintaining, on his part, the community with a person) logically (here Gogarten inserts an exclamation mark) implies the hope of forgiveness." The inference, moreover, is said to be false. "For

---

meaning to religion as religion. Hermelink seems to imply (col. 106) that authentic religion is to be found only where "the Numinous" plays the decisive role. I understand religion more simply as community with God and see Luther's "ethicizing" of religion in this, that he understood the entering into relationship with God strictly in terms of an "ought." I repeat once again: God has a *right* to demand human recognition and gratitude, and we have a *duty* to be grateful to him. This is the "deepening of the *ethical* understanding" I have in mind. And the "concept of God which is defensible on moral grounds" mentioned in my essay on Luther's doctrine of justification means no more than this—as the context indicated clearly enough—that even in justification God's truthfulness is not being violated.

6. Gogarten, "Theologie und Wissenschaft," col. 78.

the grace of God can never be inferred from the immutable severity with which he maintains his commandment as a commandment despite the fact that it cannot be fulfilled." I could reply that Gogarten here is taking issue with Luther; for Luther always did invoke a commandment as the ultimate ground of his certitude of grace; and my further exposition everywhere closely followed Luther's own remarks. But perhaps I will be allowed to add something in Luther's defense. For Luther is not appealing to just any commandment whatever, but precisely to the First Commandment. A theologian—but I would hope a layperson, too—might have noticed that its opening words, to which Luther constantly appeals ("I am the Lord, thy God"), are, according to their content, nothing other than the gospel. For that God wants to be and remain my God, despite everything—this, according to Luther, is the very quintessence of the gospel. Thus the commandment becomes a gift. It assures Luther that God still wants to have relations with him. For Luther, however, it is essential, and particularly at this very moment [in the process of justification], that the gospel, the gift of God, confronts him in the form of a commandment. If it did not lay hold of him as a divine imperative, Luther would be suspicious of himself lest his whole faith in the forgiveness of sins should have originated merely in his own will to live rather than to perish. I find that this portrayal only confirms my understanding of Luther's religion, namely, that for him religion, as an actual turning to God, rests on the sense of an "ought."

But now I, for my part, would like to address a question to Gogarten. In accordance with his understanding of the gospel—namely, that the gospel is the antithesis of every "ought"—Gogarten declares that theology can assert the distinctiveness of its subject matter only through its testimony. All right. But how do we get from the testimony of theology (and preaching) to conviction? Here Gogarten does not give us even the slightest hint. Is this no concern of theology? Does faith in this testimony arise entirely spontaneously? Perhaps because its content is so sublime, or because I am gripped by the "reality" it describes and the numinous awe that accompanies it? Is this sufficient to assure me of the truth of what is proclaimed in the gospel? Or does Gogarten share the opinion that is indeed sometimes expressed today, that the paradoxical nature of what is proclaimed is at the same time its proof? These are questions that a serious theology must answer. Otherwise theology's testimony is borne into the wind or is suspected of trying to intoxicate us by its mere pathos. Luther did answer these questions —by appealing to the conscience, to the sense of responsibility.

According to Gogarten, my reinterpretation of Luther's faith as a "fundamental moral experience" has the further necessary result that I am assigning only "secondary importance" to Christ at the heart of Luther's piety. I never used the term "secondary importance" and would never approve of another's using it. The second edition of my volume of Luther studies has shown Gogarten in the meantime what I intended to say in the places to which he refers. Even though I

115

dealt with this point in greater detail there, Gogarten nevertheless did not consider it necessary to request the publisher to return his comments and to revise the passages in question; he preferred to let his unfounded attacks on me appear in print. For when he accuses me of construing the divinity of Christ as, in principle, the same as that of human beings generally, namely, as based on their imperativistic relationship to God, with just this difference, that Jesus had complied with this imperative to a very high degree or even perfectly—against such accusations I do not care to defend myself. Let whoever attributes such views to me do it at his own risk. But it seems to me that the compulsiveness to which Gogarten refers is rather to be found on his part. He has read something similar in [Kant's] *Religion Within the Limits of Reason Alone,* and since he chose to prove the "decisive influence" of Kant on me, I was bound to agree with Kant on this point, too.

Only two points deserve further discussion in this connection. I had pointed out that Christ's receding from Luther's view in those moments of supreme *Anfechtung*[7] is also important for his Christology, especially since Luther did not impute this loss to himself as sin but rather as an *Anfechtung* imposed on him by God. Gogarten replies by asserting that, since Luther regards the whole Bible as having its meaning uniformly in Christ, those opening words of the First Commandment, ". . . thy God," refer to the same God who has revealed himself in Christ. Consequently Christ would even here be the God who helps Luther against God. Thus when Luther says clearly and distinctly of so extreme a case that Christ withdraws himself from him, or that God himself withdraws Christ from him, and that then only the First Commandment could save him, Gogarten knows better: even then it is Christ who comes to his rescue. That is what is known as letting an author say what he in fact says!

The second point has to do with Luther's Christ-mysticism. Here Gogarten stresses—I do not know whether he is attacking me or agreeing with me—that the union of the believer with Christ is not of a mystical type: "Christ does not confront the believer, he stands beside him." "The 'most substantial union' [*unio substantialissima*][8] does not

---

7. Gogarten might have saved himself the trouble of reporting (col. 74, n. 17) that he had, "without special effort," found instances where Luther says that Christ helps him in his *Anfechtung.* I had expressly referred to a gradation in Luther's *Anfechtungen,* stressing that he was ordinarily saved by Christ. I think I could produce somewhat more citations along this line than the wretched few collected by Gogarten.

8. Gogarten evidently has a closer acquaintance only with Luther's larger *Commentary on Galatians.* Many of his other Luther-citations are borrowed, and the page references are accordingly not always correct. But even the *Commentary on Galatians* is cited only in the Erlangen edition. Now I appreciate Gogarten's situation, and am always glad when someone reads Luther. But anyone who wants to enter into serious discussion about Luther simply has to use the Weimar edition, or else he must check what he has found in the Erlangen edition against the Weimar edition afterwards,

at all apply to human beings and their experience of Christ. One can even say that the fact that it is experienced is entirely irrelevant to it and to its meaning, regardless of how intimate the experience may be." "The meaning of this 'most substantial union' of human beings with Christ does not lie in its being experienced but rather in its being recognized by God as being valid. Hence everything depends on the word and therefore on faith in the word. For the word alone can signify to human beings that for God they and Christ belong together and form one loaf."

If I understand all this correctly, Gogarten is trying to say that in justification—this seems to be what is intended by the phrase "for God"—what counts is not the more or less intimate relationship of human beings to Christ but only the atoning work of Christ. Gogarten did not deem it necessary to come to grips with my exposition of Luther's doctrine of justification. What he presents is Melanchthon's doctrine, which has become part of [Lutheran] Orthodoxy: Christ is *only* the one who covers a person's sin in the sight of God. All the person has to do is to "appropriate" this righteousness of Christ through faith. I do not want to repeat here what I have just written in the *Neue kirchliche Zeitschrift* in response to Wilhelm Walther, namely, that this ostensibly Lutheran but actually Melanchthonian doctrine of justification ineluctably leads to the concept of merit. I only mention what will clarify my differences with Gogarten. In justification, Luther regards it as essential that the one with whom God—out of free grace—has entered into relationship will also actually become righteous in this relationship; otherwise God's judgment of justification would amount to a lie. To be sure, it is not a case of forming a good intention to "mend one's ways" after one has been justified; rather, God himself transforms the person within the new relationship.

Whoever understands the community with God based on justification in Luther's sense also knows that this is not merely a different way of looking at it theologically. Luther thinks he can expect a person who has been privileged to enter into community with God to be sensitive to a kind of divine pressure, and not only the pressure of God's holiness but especially the pressure of God's grace. God's instrument for transforming the person, however, is Christ. For Luther does not look upon Christ simply as the one who has atoned for the sins of humanity by his death but also at the same time as the Risen One, who is alive and at work in the hearts of believers. Luther recovered the meaning of the Pauline unity of the death and resurrection of Christ; but his recovery was slow to bear fruit within Protestantism. Melanchthon was unable to appreciate it; this is why it failed to become part of [Lutheran] Orthodoxy. But insofar as God now, in Christ, wants to draw someone ever more firmly to himself

as so many others have or had to do. Precisely in the *Commentary on Galatians* there is a very remarkable divergence between the transcription and the printed text, Luther's preface to the latter notwithstanding.

117

and to renew that person inwardly, the intimacy of the connection between Christ and the believer is not "irrelevant" in the sight of God. The more profound that intimacy becomes, the closer Christ is bringing the person to the divinely destined goal.

Luther's word against Karlstadt, quoted above, does not mean what Gogarten thinks it means. It means what Luther never ceased to preach: namely, that we cannot force the forgiveness of sins and the community with God and Christ by anything we do, however hard we might try (in the manner of the Radicals) to identify ourselves experientially with Christ. But Luther surely does not intend to bar the person to whom God freely grants this gift of community from devotion to Christ or from being transformed into the image of Christ. Luther always combines both aspects: community with God is and always remains a pure gift of grace; for the "righteousness" to which we may attain in this life is never so perfect that one could base one's confidence before God on it. And yet: something new comes about (through God) in us; God not only reprobates our works, he also always creates in us a good will. And as surely as God is the Almighty, he will finally have his way. Gogarten has a blind spot for this second element. Luther may confess as often as he will that Christ is *in* him, that as the "Lord Zabaoth" he is carrying on his warfare within him (as in every believer), that he keeps him from speaking too sharply when he is tempted to do so or that he commands him to do some particular thing—Gogarten still says: Christ only stands *beside* the believer, and that the "most substantial union" as experienced is quite irrelevant to it and to its meaning.

In all this we have already touched on the questions Gogarten treats last, which can be called Luther's ethic in the narrower sense. Since I had used the community of love in the kingdom of God as the standard in connection with the special question of the legitimacy of the state and the secular orders—I thought, quite in Luther's sense—Gogarten informs me that Luther's ethic is an "ethic of grace" based on faith rather than on love. He then sets forth a point of view that I cannot entirely put together in my own mind. Gogarten admits that there is such a thing as Luther's ethic; but the concept only appears in order to disappear again immediately. Luther's ethic is supposed to be "understandable only from the viewpoint of the critical truth of the given." Karl Barth's designation of ethics as the "great disturbance" is accordingly cited with approval, as "very instructive for the correct understanding of Luther's ethic."

As for the secular orders themselves, Gogarten tells us that Luther did not approve them because of their conformity to the commandment of love but rather because they are implanted by God. For the administration of the secular orders nothing more is required than the wisdom that was likewise implanted by God in paradise. This is said to be the very reason why Luther would like to see this task entrusted to jurists and not to theologians. For jurists would be most likely to decide such matters according to objective—"one can safely say, utili-

tarian"—criteria; and they would do their work best if they would "carry
on their work as a purely secular work, that is, not in an absolute
sense, as aiming at moral perfection, but as a thoroughly relative work,
bearing in mind the limitations of always imperfect human life." This
is supposed to show "how exceedingly close the secular stands to the
divine for Luther, despite their sharp distinction or rather because of
their sharp distinction . . . how nothing needs to be added to the
secular, nor even may be added, in order that it may become divine,
but rather that the secular must be grasped only in its pure secularity,
which in no way seeks the divine on its own, in order that it may be
grasped as the divine."

I forbear to say anything about the kind of use that is made of
Luther here. Gogarten is content to prove his case by a few passages
torn out of context. Whatever else Luther says besides is ignored.
Here, too, it is clear that Gogarten reads Luther not in order to understand him in his own terms or to learn from him, but rather in order to
gather prooftexts from his writings for views that were firmly fixed
from the outset. For my part, I really do not think that it was necessary to point out to me that Luther's ethic is an ethic of faith, an ethic
of grace. Anyone who has read even the conclusion of my essay
"What Did Luther Understand by Religion" will know that I have some
appreciation of what Romans 14:23 meant to Luther, I have also
found, however, that the God-ward side of Luther's ethic, faith, is
always intrinsically connected with the world-ward side oriented to
human beings, love. Do I really have to start citing passages in
Luther's works to the effect that the one who has been brought into
relationship with God also has a body and must have relations with
people? Must I recall the countless sermons of Luther that deal with
faith and love as the sum of Christianity?

Here Luther discovered the most difficult and complicated problems. Gogarten leaps over these problems in a way that I can only
call shocking. For his view seems to come to this: secular matters lie
so far below the faith that there is no point at all to apply to it "moral"
(i.e., absolute) standards. A utilitarian order "bearing in mind the
limitations of always imperfect human life" is alone appropriate here
—and also the will of God! For it is just then that Gogarten thinks
it becomes plain how "exceedingly close" the secular is to the divine.
And this is supposed to be the view of Luther! Did Luther never
mention that love, too, by which faith proves its effectiveness, is an
unconditional duty? Did he never say that what counts for the
Christian is not how objective his relationships are, but rather the
quality of his personal relationship to other human beings? Did he
never scold the jurists and their way of doing things? Did he never
torment himself with the question of the compatibility of the state and
the Christian law of love? Did he never offer proposals for the advancement of the secular orders in the direction of Christian love?

Luther took all these questions seriously precisely because his ethic
was an ethic of faith. But he believed in a God who not only judges

and destroys but who also creates and who establishes something eternal out of lost people in this temporal world. To be sure, here we are confronted by the most profound and ultimate riddles. I marvel at the games that are being played today with the concepts of time and eternity as though they provided answers and did not rather give rise to the most difficult theological question, namely, to what extent time is of significance for the eternal God. The theologians who have seriously thought about this problem were all ultimately confronted by the unfathomable. Caught up in time, human beings can indeed talk about this question but they cannot present anything comprehensible. This much is clear, however, and given with the Christian faith in God the Creator, that God does not undertake to do anything absurd, and that even the world and its orders must be means by which he attains his eternal goal. But then an ethic of faith which shows Christians how to fulfill their task as instruments of God is also legitimate.

It is apparent that the differences between Gogarten and myself always revolve around the same point, namely, whether the gospel is directly connected with an "ought." I want no further controversy with anyone who rejects such a connection as constituting a relapse into imperativism, that is, who takes the gift [of God] without any sense of being put thereby in any way in God's debt. In any case, such an attitude has nothing to do with Luther's. But I assume that actually Gogarten himself cannot inwardly sustain the kind of "stance of faith" he describes. There are theologians who are better than their theology. I would like to think that Gogarten is one of them.[9]

---

9. Editors' Note: The German text of Holl's reply to Gogarten is entitled "Gogartens Lutherauffassung: Eine Erwiderung"; the reply is found in GA 3, pp. 244–253. The reply was published originally in Die Christliche Welt 38 (1924): cols. 307–14. The English translation is by Walter F. Bense.

Indexes

Index of Names

121

Index of Subjects